362.4 America

The Americans with Disabilities
Act (ADA) : provisions and
protections

THE AMERICANS WITH DISABILITIES ACT (ADA)

PROVISIONS AND PROTECTIONS

DISABILITY AND THE DISABLED-ISSUES, LAWS AND PROGRAMS

Additional books in this series can be found on Nova's website
under the Series tab.

Additional E-books in this series can be found on Nova's website
under the E-book tab.

THE AMERICANS WITH DISABILITIES ACT (ADA)

PROVISIONS AND PROTECTIONS

John Kiviniemi
and
Cécile Sanjo
EDITORS

Nova Science Publishers, Inc.
New York

Library of Congress Cataloging-in-Publication Data

Jones, Nancy Lee.
  The Americans with Disabilities Act (ADA) : provisions and protections / editors, John Kiviniemi and Cicile Sanjo.
     p. cm.
  Includes index.
  Consists of CRS Reports for Congress
  ISBN 978-1-61470-961-9 (hardcover)
  1. United States. Americans with Disabilities Act of 1990. 2. People with disabilities--Legal status, laws, etc.--United States. I. Toland, Carol J. II. Kiviniemi, John. III. Sanjo, Cicile. IV. Title.
  KF480.A25 2011
  342.7308'7--dc23
                          2011028728

Published by Nova Science Publishers, Inc. † New York

CONTENTS

PREFACE

Chapter 1- The Americans with Disabilities Act (ADA) provides broad nondiscrimination protection in employment, public services, public accommodations, services operated by public entities, transportation, and telecommunications for individuals with disabilities. This report summarizes the major provisions of the ADA and analyzes selected recent issues, including the Supreme Court cases and the ADA Amendments Act of 2008.

Chapter 2- The Americans with Disabilities Act (ADA) is a broad civil rights act prohibiting discrimination against individuals with disabilities. As stated in the act, its purpose is "to provide a clear and comprehensive national mandate for the elimination of discrimination against individuals with disabilities."

Chapter 3- The Americans with Disabilities Act (ADA) has as its purpose "to provide a clear and comprehensive national mandate for the elimination of discrimination against individuals with disabilities." On July 26, 2010, the 20th anniversary of the passage of the ADA, the Department of Justice (DOJ) issued final rules amending the existing regulations under ADA title II (prohibiting discrimination against individuals with disabilities by state and local governments) and ADA title III (prohibiting discrimination against individuals with disabilities by places of public accommodations). The new regulations for title II and title III are similar. They both adopt accessibility standards consistent with the minimum guidelines and requirements issued by the Architectural and Transportation Barriers Compliance Board (Access Board). In addition, the regulations include more detailed standards for service animals and power-driven mobility devices, ticketing, effective communication, and provide for an element-by-element "safe harbor" in certain circumstances. The regulations take effect March 15, 2011, but compliance with the 2010 standards for accessible design is not required until March 15, 2012. These final regulations only address issues that were in the 2008 notice of proposed rulemaking. DOJ has noted that it intends to engage in additional rulemaking in certain areas, including equipment and furniture, next generation 9-1-1, movie captioning and video description, and accessibility of websites operated by public entities or places of public accommodation.

Chapter 4- The ADA Amendment Act (ADAAA), P.L. 110-325, was enacted in 2008 to amend the Americans with Disabilities Act (ADA) definition of disability. On March 25, 2011, the Equal Employment Opportunity Commission (EEOC) issued final regulations implementing the ADAAA. The final regulations track the statutory language of the ADA but also provide several clarifying interpretations. Several of the major regulatory interpretations are, including the operation of major bodily functions in the definition of major life activities;

adding rules of construction for when an impairment substantially limits a major life activity and providing examples of impairments that will most often be found to substantially limit a major life activity; interpreting the coverage of transitory impairments; interpreting the use of mitigating measures; and interpreting the "regarded as" prong of the definition.

Chapter 5- The Americans with Disabilities Act (ADA) provides broad nondiscrimination protection in employment, public services, and public accommodation and services operated by private entities. Since the 106th Congress, legislation has been introduced to require plaintiffs to provide notice to the defendant prior to filing a complaint regarding public accommodations. In the 112th Congress, H.R. 881 was introduced by Representative Hunter to amend Title III of the ADA to require notification.

Chapter 6- The Americans with Disabilities Act (ADA) provides broad nondiscrimination protection for individuals with disabilities in employment, public services, and public accommodations and services operated by private entities. Although the ADA does not include provisions specifically discussing its application to disasters, its nondiscrimination provisions are applicable to emergency preparedness and responses to disasters. In order to further the ADA's goals, President Bush issued an Executive Order on July 22, 2004, relating to emergency preparedness for individuals with disabilities and establishing the Interagency Coordinating Council on Emergency Preparedness and Individuals with Disabilities. The Department of Homeland Security (DHS) issued its Nationwide Plan Review Phase 2 Report, which includes a discussion of people with disabilities and emergency planning and readiness. The National Council on Disability has also issued recommendations on emergency preparation and disaster relief relating to individuals with disabilities. The Post-Katrina Emergency Management Reform Act of 2006 added the position of disability coordinator to FEMA.

Chapter 7- The Americans with Disabilities Act (ADA) provides broad nondiscrimination protection for individuals with disabilities in employment, public services, and public accommodations and services operated by private entities. Although the ADA does not include provisions specifically discussing its application to disasters, its nondiscrimination provisions are applicable to emergency preparedness and responses to disasters. In order to further the ADA's goals, President Bush issued an Executive Order on July 22, 2004, relating to emergency preparedness for individuals with disabilities and establishing the Interagency Coordinating Council on Emergency Preparedness and Individuals with Disabilities. The Department of Homeland Security (DHS) issued its Nationwide Plan Review Phase 2 Report, which includes a discussion of people with disabilities and emergency planning and readiness. The National Council on Disability has also issued recommendations on emergency preparation and disaster relief relating to individuals with disabilities. The Post-Katrina Emergency Management Reform Act of 2006 added the position of disability coordinator to FEMA.

Chapter 8- The Americans with Disabilities Act (ADA), 42 U.S.C. §§12101 *et seq.,* provides broad nondiscrimination protection for individuals with disabilities in employment, public services, public accommodations and services operated by private entities, transportation, and telecommunications. As stated in the act, its purpose is "to provide a clear and comprehensive national mandate for the elimination of discrimination against individuals with disabilities." Due to concern about the spread of highly contagious diseases such as pandemic influenza and extensively drug-resistant tuberculosis (XDR-TB), questions have been raised about the application of the ADA in such situations. Generally, individuals with serious contagious diseases would most likely be considered individuals with disabilities. However, this does not mean that an individual with a serious contagious disease would have to be hired or given access to a place of public accommodation if such an action would place other individuals at a significant risk. Such determinations are highly fact specific and the differences between the contagious diseases may give rise to differing conclusions since each contagious disease has specific patterns of transmission that affect the magnitude and duration of a potential threat to others.

Chapter 9- The Americans with Disabilities Act (ADA) provides broad nondiscrimination protection in employment, public services, public accommodations, and services operated by private entities, transportation, and telecommunications for individuals with disabilities. As stated in the act, its purpose is "to provide a clear and comprehensive national mandate for the elimination of discrimination against individuals with disabilities."

Chapter 10- The Americans with Disabilities Act (ADA) is a broad civil rights statute prohibiting discrimination against individuals with disabilities. Title III of the ADA prohibits discrimination by public accommodations, which are defined to include movie theaters, but the statute does not include specific language on closed captioning or video description. Although the Department of Justice (DOJ) has promulgated regulations under Title III, it has not specifically addressed issues regarding closed captioning or video description. However, DOJ has issued an advance notice of proposed rulemaking (ANPR) to establish requirements for closed captioning and video description for movie theaters. The ANPR asks for input in several areas including the implications of a sliding compliance schedule, and the appropriate basis for calculating the number of movies that will be captioned and video described. In addition, the Ninth Circuit, in the first court of appeals case to address the issue, held that the ADA requires the provision of closed captioning and descriptive narration in movie theaters unless to do so would be a fundamental alteration or an undue burden.

Chapter 11- The Americans with Disabilities Act (ADA) has as its purpose providing "a clear and comprehensive national mandate for the elimination of discrimination against individuals with disabilities." In order to effectuate this purpose, the ADA and its regulations require reasonable accommodation or modifications in policies, practices, or procedures when such modifications are necessary to render the goods, services, facilities, privileges, advantages, or accommodations accessible to individuals with disabilities. The reasonable accommodation or modification requirement has been interpreted to allow the use of service animals, even in places where animals are generally not permitted.

Chapter 12- The Americans with Disabilities Act (ADA) has as its purpose providing "a clear and comprehensive national mandate for the elimination of discrimination against individuals with disabilities." In order to effectuate this purpose, the ADA and its regulations require reasonable accommodation or modifications in policies, practices, or procedures when such modifications are necessary to render the goods, services, facilities, privileges, advantages, or accommodations accessible to individuals with disabilities. The reasonable accommodation or modification requirement has been interpreted to allow the use of service animals, even in places where animals are generally not permitted.

Chapter 13- State law generally governs parking privileges for people with disabilities. However, federal regulations offer a uniform system of parking privileges, which includes model definitions and rules regarding license plates and placards, parking and parking space design, and interstate reciprocity. The federal government encourages states to adopt this uniform system. As a result, most states have incorporated at least some aspects of the uniform regulations into their handicapped parking laws. This report describes the federal role in parking privileges law, outlines the uniform system's model rules, and briefly discusses state responses to the model federal rules.

In: The Americans with Disabilities Act (ADA): Provisions...   ISBN: 978-1-61470-961-9
Editor: John Kiviniemi and Cécile Sanjo   © 2012 Nova Science Publishers, Inc.

Chapter 1

THE AMERICANS WITH DISABILITIES ACT (ADA): STATUTORY LANGUAGE AND RECENT ISSUES

Nancy Lee Jones

SUMMARY

The Americans with Disabilities Act (ADA) provides broad nondiscrimination protection in employment, public services, public accommodations, services operated by public entities, transportation, and telecommunications for individuals with disabilities. This report summarizes the major provisions of the ADA and analyzes selected recent issues, including the Supreme Court cases and the ADA Amendments Act of 2008.

BACKGROUND

The Americans with Disabilities Act, ADA, 42 U.S.C. §§12101 *et seq.*, has often been described as the most sweeping nondiscrimination legislation since the Civil Rights Act of 1964. It provides broad nondiscrimination protection in employment, public services, public accommodations, and services operated by private entities, transportation, and telecommunications for individuals with disabilities.[1] As stated in the act, its purpose is "to provide a clear and comprehensive national mandate for the elimination of discrimination against individuals with disabilities." Enacted on July 26, 1990, the majority of the ADA's provisions took effect in 1992.[2] The ADA Amendments Act, P.L. 110-325, was enacted on September 25, 2008, to respond to a series of Supreme Court decisions that had interpreted the definition of disability narrowly.[3]

The Supreme Court has decided 20 ADA cases.[4] In the most recent Supreme Court decision, *United States v. Georgia*,[5] the Court held that Title II of the ADA created a private cause of action for damages against the states for conduct that actually violated the Fourteenth Amendment. However, the Court did not reach the issue of whether the Eleventh Amendment permits a prisoner to secure money damages from a state for state actions that violate the

ADA but not the Constitution. In addition, the Supreme Court decided *Arbaugh v. Y. & H Corp.*,[6] a case under Title VII of the Civil Rights Act of 1964, which has implications for the ADA's prohibition of discrimination where employers employ 15 or more employees.

On December 7, 2007, the Supreme Court granted certiorari in *Huber v. Wal-Mart Stores,*[7] to determine whether an individual with a disability who cannot perform her current job must be reassigned to a vacant, equivalent position without competing with other workers. However, the Court dismissed the petition since the case was settled prior to oral argument. Currently, there is a split in the circuits on this accommodation issue, and in light of the Court's dismissal of the case, there will continue to be divergent views.[8]

Before examining the provisions of the ADA and these cases, it is important to briefly note the ADA's historical antecedents. A federal statutory provision which existed prior to the ADA, Section 504 of the Rehabilitation Act of 1973, prohibits discrimination against an otherwise qualified individual with a disability, solely on the basis of the disability, in any program or activity that receives federal financial assistance, the executive agencies or the U.S. Postal Service.[9] Many of the concepts used in the ADA originated in Section 504 and its interpretations; however, there is one major difference. While Section 504's prohibition against discrimination is tied to the receipt of federal financial assistance, the ADA also covers entities not receiving such funds. In addition, the federal executive agencies and the U.S. Postal Service are covered under Section 504, not the ADA. The ADA contains a specific provision stating that except as otherwise provided in the act, nothing in the act shall be construed to apply a lesser standard than the standards applied under Title V of the Rehabilitation Act (which includes Section 504) or the regulations issued by federal agencies pursuant to such Title.[10]

The ADA is a civil rights statute; it does not provide grant funds to help entities comply with its requirements. It does include a section on technical assistance which authorizes grants and awards for the purpose of technical assistance such as the dissemination of information about rights under the ADA and techniques for effective compliance.[11] However, there are tax code provisions which may assist certain businesses or individuals.[12]

DEFINITION OF DISABILITY

Statutory Language

Definition Language

The definitions in the ADA, particularly the definition of "disability," are the starting point for an analysis of rights provided by the law.[13] The term "disability," with respect to an individual, is defined as "(A) a physical or mental impairment that substantially limits one or more of the major life activities of such individual; (B) a record of such an impairment; or (C) being regarded as having such an impairment (as described in paragraph (3))."[14] The definition of disability was the subject of numerous cases brought under the ADA including major Supreme Court decisions which generally interpreted the definition narrowly. Due to these interpretations, Congress enacted the ADA Amendments Act, which kept essentially the same statutory language but contains new rules of construction regarding the definition of disability. These rules of construction provide that

- the definition of disability shall be construed in favor of broad coverage to the maximum extent permitted by the terms of the act;
- the term "substantially limits" shall be interpreted consistently with the findings and purposes of the ADA Amendments Act;
- an impairment that substantially limits one major life activity need not limit other major life activities to be considered a disability;
- an impairment that is episodic or in remission is a disability if it would have substantially limited a major life activity when active;
- the determination of whether an impairment substantially limits a major life activity shall be made without regard to the ameliorative effects of mitigating measures, except that the ameliorative effects of ordinary eyeglasses or contact lenses shall be considered.[15]

The final EEOC regulations track the statutory definition but also provide some clarifying interpretations. For example, the operation of major bodily functions is included in the definition of major life activities. In addition, although the EEOC emphasizes the ADAAA's requirement for an individualized assessment, the regulations list some impairments that will almost always be determined to be a disability. These include deafness, blindness, an intellectual disability, missing limbs or mobility impairments requiring the use of a wheelchair, autism, cancer, cerebral palsy, diabetes, epilepsy, HIV infection, multiple sclerosis, muscular dystrophy, major depressive disorder, bipolar disorder, post-traumatic stress disorder, obsessive compulsive disorder, and schizophrenia.[16]

Statement of Findings and Purposes Regarding the Definition
The findings of the ADA Amendments Act include statements indicating that the Supreme Court decisions in *Sutton v. United Air Lines, Inc.*,[17] and *Toyota Motor Manufacturing v. Williams*[18] as well as lower court cases have narrowed and limited the ADA from what was intended by Congress. The codified findings in the original ADA are amended to delete the finding that "43,000,000 Americans have one or more physical or mental disabilities...." This finding was used in *Sutton* to support limiting the reach of the definition of disability. P.L. 110-325 specifically states that the current EEOC regulations defining the term "substantially limits" as "significantly restricted" are "inconsistent with congressional intent, by expressing too high a standard." The EEOC has promulgated regulations under the ADA Amendments Act which change the definition of "substantially limits."[19]

The ADA Amendments Act states that the purposes of the legislation are to carry out the ADA's objectives of the elimination of discrimination and the provision of "'clear, strong, consistent, enforceable standards addressing discrimination' by reinstating a broad scope of protection available under the ADA." P.L. 110-325 rejected the Supreme Court's holdings that mitigating measures are to be used in making a determination of whether an impairment substantially limits a major life activity as well as holdings defining the "substantially limits" requirements. The substantially limits requirements of *Toyota* as well as the former EEOC regulations defining substantially limits as "significantly restricted" are specifically rejected in the new law.

Major Life Activities

The ADA Amendments Act specifically lists examples of major life activities including caring for oneself, performing manual tasks, seeing, hearing, eating, sleeping, walking, standing, lifting, bending, speaking, breathing, learning, reading, concentrating, thinking, communicating, and working. The act also states that a major life activity includes the operation of a major bodily function. The House Judiciary Committee report indicates that "this clarification was needed to ensure that the impact of an impairment on the operation of major bodily functions is not overlooked or wrongly dismissed as falling outside the definition of 'major life activities' under the ADA."[20] There had been judicial decisions which found that certain bodily functions had not been covered by the definition of disability. For example, in *Furnish v. SVI Sys., Inc.,*[21] the Seventh Circuit held that an individual with cirrhosis of the liver due to infection with Hepatitis B was not an individual with a disability because liver function was not "integral to one's daily existence."

Regarded as Having a Disability

The third prong of the definition of disability covers individuals who are "regarded as having such an impairment (as described in paragraph (3))." Paragraph 3 states that "[a]n individual meets the requirement of 'being regarded as having such an impairment' if the individual establishes that he or she has been subjected to an action prohibited under this Act because of an actual or perceived physical or mental impairment whether or not the impairment limits or is perceived to limit a major life activity." However, impairments that are transitory and minor are specifically excluded from the regarded prong. A transitory impairment is one with an actual or expected duration of six months or less. The ADA Amendments Act also provides in a rule of construction in Title V of the ADA that a covered entity under Title I,[22] a public entity under Title II, or a person who operates a place of public accommodation under Title III, need not provide a reasonable accommodation or a reasonable modification to policies, practices, or procedures to an individual who meets the definition of disability solely under the "regarded as" prong of the definition.

Regulatory Authority to Promulgate Regulations Regarding the Definition of Disability

The Supreme Court in *Sutton* questioned the authority of regulatory agencies to promulgate regulations for the definition of disability in the ADA. The definition of disability is contained in Section 3 of the ADA, and the ADA does not specifically give any agency the authority to interpret the definitions in Section 3, including the definition of disability. The Supreme Court declined to address this issue since, as both parties to *Sutton* accepted the regulation as valid, "we have no occasion to consider what deference they are due, if any." The ADA Amendments Act specifically grants regulatory authority and states that "[t]he authority to issue regulations granted to the Equal Employment Opportunity Commission, the Attorney General, and the Secretary of Transportation under this Act, includes the authority to issue regulations implementing the definitions contained in sections 3 and 4."

Title V Provisions on the Definition of Disability

The definition of "disability" was further elaborated in Title V of the ADA. Section 510 provides that the term "individual with a disability" in the ADA does not include an individual who is currently engaging in the illegal use of drugs when the covered entity acts on the basis of such use.[23] An individual who has been rehabilitated would be covered. However, the conference report language clarifies that the provision does not permit individuals to invoke coverage simply by showing they are participating in a drug rehabilitation program; they must refrain from using drugs.[24] The conference report also indicates that the limitation in coverage is not intended to be narrowly construed to only persons who use drugs "on the day of, or within a matter of weeks before, the action in question."[25] The definitional section of the Rehabilitation Act was also amended to create uniformity with this definition.

Section 508 provides that an individual shall not be considered to have a disability solely because that individual is a transvestite.[26] Section 511 similarly provides that homosexuality and bisexuality are not disabilities under the act and that the term disability does not include transvestism, transsexualism, pedophilia, exhibitionism, voyeurism, gender identity disorders not resulting from physical impairments, or other sexual behavior disorders, compulsive gambling, kleptomania, or pyromania, or psychoactive substance use disorders resulting from current illegal use of drugs.[27]

Supreme Court Cases

The Supreme Court has decided several cases relating to the definition of disability. The first ADA case to address the definitional issue was *Bragdon v. Abbott*, a case involving a dentist who refused to treat an HIV infected individual outside of a hospital.[28] In *Bragdon,* the Court found that the plaintiff's asymptomatic HIV infection was a physical impairment impacting on the major life activity of reproduction thus rending HIV infection a disability under the ADA. The other decisions—*Sutton v. United Airlines,*[29] *Murphy v. United Parcel Service, Inc.,*[30] *Albertsons Inc. v. Kirkingburg,*[31] and *Toyota Motor Manufacturing v. Williams*[32]—all involved issues which Congress later addressed in the ADA Amendments Act. Thus, although these decisions are of historical interest, especially regarding the impetus for the enactment of the ADA Amendments Act, they can no longer be assumed to be valid precedent and therefore will only be briefly discussed here.

Bragdon v. Abbott

The Supreme Court in *Bragdon v. Abbott* addressed the ADA definition of individual with a disability and held that the respondent's asymptomatic HIV infection was a physical impairment impacting on the major life activity of reproduction thus rendering the HIV infection a disability under the ADA.[33] In 1994, Dr. Bragdon performed a dental examination on Ms. Abbott and discovered a cavity. Ms. Abbott had indicated in her registration form that she was HIV positive but at that time she was asymptomatic. Dr. Bragdon told her that he would not fill her cavity in his office but would treat her only in a hospital setting. Ms. Abbott filed an ADA complaint and prevailed at the district court, courts of appeals and the Supreme Court on the issue of whether she was an individual with a disability but the case was remanded for further consideration regarding the issue of direct threat.

In arriving at its holding, Justice Kennedy, writing for the majority, first looked to whether Ms. Abbott's HIV infection was a physical impairment. Noting the immediacy with which the HIV virus begins to damage an individual's white blood cells, the Court found that asymptomatic HIV infection was a physical impairment. Second, the Court examined whether this physical impairment affected a major life activity and concluded that the HIV infection placed a substantial limitation on her ability to reproduce and to bear children and that reproduction was a major life activity. Finally, the Court examined whether the physical impairment was a substantial limitation on the major life activity of reproduction. After evaluating the medical evidence, the Court concluded that Ms. Abbott's ability to reproduce was substantially limited in two ways: (1) an attempt to conceive would impose a significant risk on Ms. Abbott's partner, and (2) an HIV infected woman risks infecting her child during gestation and childbirth.[34]

Sutton v. United Airlines, Murphy v. United Parcel Service, and Albertsons, Inc. v Kirkingburg

Three Supreme Court decisions in 1999 addressed the definition of disability and specifically discussed the concept of mitigating measures. *Sutton v. United Air Lines* involved sisters who were rejected from employment as pilots with United Air Lines because they wore eyeglasses. The Supreme Court in *Sutton* examined the definition of disability used in the original ADA and found that the determination of whether an individual has a disability should be made with reference to measures that mitigate the individual's impairment. The *Sutton* Court stated: "'a disability' exists only where an impairment 'substantially limits' a major life activity, not where it 'might,' 'could,' or 'would' be substantially limiting if mitigating measures were not taken." The Court also emphasized that the statement of findings in the ADA that some 43,000,000 Americans have one or more physical or mental disability "requires the conclusion that Congress did not intend to bring under the statute's protection all those whose uncorrected conditions amount to disabilities."

Similarly, in *Murphy v. United Parcel Service, Inc.*, the Court held that the fact that an individual with high blood pressure was unable to meet the Department of Transportation (DOT) safety standards was not sufficient to create an issue of fact regarding whether an individual is regarded as unable to utilize a class of jobs. The Court in *Murphy* found that an employee is regarded as having a disability if the covered entity mistakenly believes that the employee's actual, nonlimiting impairment substantially limits one or more major life activities. And in the last of this trilogy of 1999 cases, the Court in *Albertsons v. Kirkingburg* held that a trucker with monocular vision who was able to compensate for this impairment was not a person with a disability.

Toyota Motor Manufacturing of Kentucky v. Williams

In the 2002 case of *Toyota Motor Manufacturing v. Williams,* the meaning of "substantially limits" was examined, and Justice O'Connor, writing for the unanimous Court, determined that the word substantial "clearly precluded impairments that interfere in only a minor way with the performance of manual tasks." The Court also found that the term "major life activity" "refers to those activities that are of central importance to daily life." Finding that these terms are to be "interpreted strictly," the Court held that "to be substantially limited in performing manual tasks, an individual must have an impairment that prevents or severely restricts the individual from doing activities that are of central importance to most people's daily lives."

APPLICATION OF THE ELEVENTH AMENDMENT TO THE ADA

The Eleventh Amendment states: "The Judicial power of the United States shall not be construed to extend to any suit in law or equity, commenced or prosecuted against one of the United States by Citizens of another State, or by Citizens or Subjects of any Foreign State." The Supreme Court has found that the Eleventh Amendment cannot be abrogated by the use of Article I powers but that Section 5 of the Fourteenth Amendment can be used for abrogation in certain circumstances. Section 5 of the Fourteenth Amendment states: "The Congress shall have the power to enforce, by appropriate legislation, the provisions of this article."

The circumstances where Section 5 of the Fourteenth Amendment can be used to abrogate the Eleventh Amendment were discussed in the Supreme Court decisions in *College Savings Bank v. Florida Prepaid Postsecondary Educ. Expense Board*,[35] *Florida Prepaid Postsecondary Educ. Expense Board v. College Savings Bank*,[36] and *Kimel v. Florida Board of Regents*.[37] They reiterated the principle that the Congress may abrogate state immunity from suit under the Fourteenth Amendment and found that there were three conditions necessary for successful abrogation.

- Congressional power is limited to the enactment of "appropriate" legislation to enforce the substantive provisions of the Fourteenth Amendment.
- The legislation must be remedial in nature.
- There must be a "congruence and proportionality" between the injury to be prevented and the means adopted to that end.

The ADA uses both the Fourteenth Amendment and the Commerce Clause of the Constitution as its constitutional basis.[38] It also specifically abrogates state immunity under the Eleventh Amendment.[39] The ADA, then, is clear regarding its attempt to abrogate state immunity; the issue is whether the other elements of a successful abrogation are present. The Supreme Court in *Garrett v. University of Alabama* found that they were not with regard to Title I while in *Tennessee v. Lane* the Court upheld Title II as it applies to the access to courts.[40] Most recently, the Supreme Court in *United States v. Georgia*,[41] held that Title II of the ADA created a private cause of action for damages against the states for conduct that actually violates the Fourteenth Amendment. However, the Court did not reach the issue of whether the Eleventh Amendment permits a prisoner to secure money damages from a state for state actions that violate the ADA but not the Constitution.

EMPLOYMENT

General Requirements

Statutory and Regulatory Requirements

Title I of the ADA, as amended by the ADA Amendments Act of 2008, provides that no covered entity shall discriminate against a qualified individual on the basis of disability in regard to job application procedures, the hiring, advancement, or discharge of employees, employee compensation, job training, and other terms, conditions, and privileges of employment.[42] The term *employer* is defined as a person engaged in an industry affecting commerce who has 15 or more employees.[43] Therefore, the employment section of the ADA, unlike the section on public accommodations, which will be discussed subsequently, is limited in scope to employers with 15 or more employees. This parallels the coverage provided in the Civil Rights Act of 1964. As noted previously, the Supreme Court, in *Arbaugh v. Y. & H. Corp.*,[44] held that the 15-employee limitation in Title VII of the Civil Rights Act[45] was not jurisdictional, but rather was related to the substantive adequacy of a claim. Thus, if the defense that the employer employs fewer than 15 employees is not raised in a timely manner, a court is not obligated to dismiss the case. Because the ADA's 15-employee limitation language parallels that of Title VII, it is likely that a court would interpret the ADA's requirement in the same manner.

The term *employee* with respect to employment in a foreign country includes an individual who is a citizen of the United States; however, it is not unlawful for a covered entity to take action that constitutes discrimination with respect to an employee in a workplace in a foreign country if compliance would cause the covered entity to violate the law of the foreign country.[46]

If the issue raised under the ADA is employment related, and the threshold issues of meeting the definition of an individual with a disability and involving an employer employing more than 15 individuals are met, the next step is to determine whether the individual is a qualified individual with a disability who, with or without reasonable accommodation, can perform the essential functions of the job.

Title I defines a "qualified individual with a disability." Such an individual is "an individual with a disability who, with or without reasonable accommodation, can perform the essential functions of the employment position that such person holds or desires."[47] The ADA incorporates many of the concepts set forth in the regulations promulgated pursuant to Section 504, including the requirement to provide reasonable accommodation unless the accommodation would pose an undue hardship on the operation of the business.[48]

"Reasonable accommodation" is defined in the ADA as including making existing facilities readily accessible to and usable by individuals with disabilities, and job restructuring, part-time or modified work schedules, reassignment to a vacant position, acquisition or modification of equipment or devices, adjustment of examinations or training materials or policies, provision of qualified readers or interpreters or other similar accommodations.[49] "Undue hardship" is defined as "an action requiring significant difficulty or expense."[50] Factors to be considered in determining whether an action would create an undue hardship include the nature and cost of the accommodation, the overall financial resources of the facility, the overall financial resources of the covered entity, and the type of operation or operations of the covered entity.

Reasonable accommodation and the related concept of undue hardship are significant concepts under the ADA and are one of the major ways in which the ADA is distinguishable from Title VII jurisprudence. The statutory language paraphrased above provides some guidance for employers but the details of the requirements have been the subject of numerous judicial decisions. In addition, the EEOC issued detailed enforcement guidance on these concepts on March 1, 1999,[51] which was amended on October 17, 2002, to reflect the Supreme Court's decision in *U.S. Airways v. Barnett*.[52] Although much of the guidance reiterates longstanding EEOC interpretations in a question and answer format, the EEOC also took issue with some judicial interpretations.[53] Notably the EEOC stated that

- an employee who is granted leave as a reasonable accommodation is entitled to return to his or her same position, unless this imposes an undue hardship; and
- an employer is limited in the ability to question the employee's documentation of a disability ("An employer cannot ask for documentation when: (1) both the disability and the need for reasonable accommodation are obvious, or (2) the individual has already provided the employer with sufficient information to substantiate that s/he has an ADA disability and needs the reasonable accommodation requested.").

Issues regarding the amount of money that must be spent on reasonable accommodations have also arisen. The EEOC regulations[54] and guidance provide that an employer does not have to provide a reasonable accommodation that would cause an "undue hardship" to the employer.[55] However, the Seventh Circuit in *Vande Zande v. State of Wisconsin Department of Administration*[56] found that the cost of the accommodation cannot be disproportionate to the benefit. "Even if an employer is so large or wealthy—or, like the principal defendant in this case, is a state, which can raise taxes in order to finance any accommodations that it must make to disabled employees—that it may not be able to plead 'undue hardship', it would not be required to expend enormous sums in order to bring about a trivial improvement in the life of a disabled employee."[57]

Clackamas Gastroenterology Associates P.C. v. Wells

The Supreme Court examined the definition of the term "employee" under the ADA in *Clackamas Gastroenterology Associates P.C. v. Wells.*[58] In *Clackamas,* the Court held in a 7-2 decision written by Justice Stevens, that the EEOC's guidelines concerning whether a shareholder-director is an employee were the correct standard to use. Since the evidence was not clear, the case was remanded for further proceedings. Clackamas Gastroenterology Associates is a medical clinic in Oregon that employed Ms. Wells as a bookkeeper from 1986-1997. After her termination from employment, Ms. Wells brought an action alleging unlawful discrimination on the basis of discrimination under Title I of the ADA. The clinic denied that it was covered by the ADA since it argued that it did not have 15 or more employees for the 20 weeks per year required by the statute. The determination of coverage was dependent on whether the four physician-shareholders who owned the professional corporation were counted as employees.

The Court first looked to the definition of employee in the ADA which states that an employee is "an individual employed by an employer."[59] This definition was described as one which is "completely circular and explains nothing." The majority then looked to common law, specifically the common law element of control. This is the position advocated by the EEOC. The EEOC has issued guidelines which list six factors to be considered in determining whether the individual acts independently and participates in managing the organization or whether the individual is subject to the organization's control and therefore an employee. These six factors are:

Whether the organization can hire or fire the individual or set the rules and regulations of the individual's work; Whether and, if so, to what extent the organization supervises the individual's work; Whether the individual reports to someone higher in the organization; Whether and, if so, to what extent the individual is able to influence the organization; Whether the parties intended that the individual be an employee, as expressed in written agreements or contracts; and Whether the individual shares in the profits, losses, and liabilities of the organization.[60]

Justice Stevens, writing for the majority, found that some of the district court's findings of fact, when considered in light of the EEOC's standard, appeared to favor the conclusion that the four physicians were not employees of the clinic. However, since there was some evidence that might support the opposite conclusion, the Court remanded the case for further proceedings.

Justice Ginsburg, joined by Justice Breyer, dissented from the majority's opinion. The dissenters argued that the Court's opinion used only one of the common-law aspects of a master-servant relationship. In addition, Justice Ginsburg noted that the physician-shareholders argued they were employees for the purposes of other statutes, notably the Employee Retirement Income Security Act of 1974 (ERISA) and stated "I see no reason to allow the doctors to escape from their choice of corporate form when the question becomes whether they are employees for the purposes of federal antidiscrimination statutes."

Other Supreme Court Employment Cases

Many of the Supreme Court decisions have involved employment situations although a number of these cases did not reach past the threshold issue of whether the individual alleging employment discrimination was an individual with a disability. There are still several significant employment issues, such as reasonable accommodations, which have not been dealt with by the Court. In addition, the landmark decision of *University of Alabama v. Garrett* on the application of the Eleventh Amendment arose in the employment context.

Receipt of SSI Benefits
The relationship between the receipt of SSDI benefits and the ability of an individual to pursue an ADA employment claim was the issue in *Cleveland v. Policy Management Systems Corp, supra*. The Supreme Court unanimously held that pursuit and receipt of SSDI benefits does not automatically stop a recipient from pursuing an ADA claim or even create a strong presumption against success under the ADA. Observing that the Social Security Act and the ADA both help individuals with disabilities but in different ways, the Court found that "despite the appearance of conflict that arises from the language of the two statutes, the two claims do not inherently conflict to the point where courts should apply a special negative presumption like the one applied by the Court of Appeals here." The fact that the ADA defines a qualified individual as one who can perform the essential functions of the job with or without reasonable accommodation was seen as a key distinction between the ADA and the Social Security Act. In addition, the Court observed that SSDI benefits are sometimes granted to individuals who are working.

The Seventh Circuit, in *Johnson v. ExxonmobilCorp.,*[61] applied the Supreme Court's analysis in *Cleveland* and distinguished the factual situations. In *Cleveland* the plaintiff had argued that she had made consistent statements in her ADA claim and in the SSDI application; however, in *Johnson* the Seventh Circuit found that the plaintiff had merely argued that "he was mistaken in his SSDI application." The court of appeals concluded that "*Cleveland* does not stand for the proposition that defendants should be allowed to explain why they gave false statements on their SSDI applications, which is essentially what Johnson seeks to do here."[62]

"Qualified" Individual with a Disability

In *Albertsons, Inc. v. Kirkingburg*,[63] the Supreme Court held that an employer need not adopt an experimental vision waiver program. Title I of the ADA prohibits discrimination in employment against a "qualified" individual with a disability. In finding that the plaintiff's inability to comply with the general regulatory vision requirements rendered him unqualified, the Court framed the question in the following manner. "Is it reasonable ... to read the ADA as requiring an employer like Albertsons to shoulder the general statutory burden to justify a job qualification that would tend to exclude the disabled, whenever the employer chooses to abide by the otherwise clearly applicable, unamended substantive regulatory standard despite the Government's willingness to waive it experimentally and without any finding of its being inappropriate?" Answering this question in the negative, the Court observed that employers should not be required to "reinvent the Government's own wheel" and stated that "it is simply not credible that Congress enacted the ADA (before there was any waiver program) with the understanding that employers choosing to respect the Government's sole substantive visual acuity regulation in the face of an experimental waiver might be burdened with an obligation to defend the regulation's application according to its own terms."

In *Chevron U.S.A. Inc., v. Echazabal*,[64] the Supreme Court held unanimously that the ADA does not require an employer to hire an individual with a disability if the job in question would endanger the individual's health. The ADA's statutory language provides for a defense to an allegation of discrimination that a qualification standard is "job related and consistent with business necessity."[65] The act also allows an employer to impose as a qualification standard that the individual shall not pose a direct threat to the health or safety of other individuals in the workplace[66] but does not discuss a threat to the individual's health or safety. The Ninth Circuit in *Echazabal* had determined that an employer violated the ADA by refusing to hire an applicant with a serious liver condition whose illness would be aggravated through exposure to the chemicals in the workplace.[67] The Supreme Court rejected the Ninth Circuit decision and upheld a regulation by the EEOC that allows an employer to assert a direct threat defense to an allegation of employment discrimination where the threat is posed only to the health or safety of the individual making the allegation.[68] Justice Souter found that the EEOC regulations were not the kind of workplace paternalism that the ADA seeks to outlaw. "The EEOC was certainly acting within the reasonable zone when it saw a difference between rejecting workplace paternalism and ignoring specific and documented risks to the employee himself, even if the employee would take his chances for the sake of getting a job." The Court emphasized that a direct threat defense must be based on medical judgment that uses the most current medical knowledge.

The Supreme Court had examined an analogous issue in *UAW v. Johnson Controls, Inc.*,[69] which held that under the Civil Rights Act of 1964 employers could not enforce "fetal protection" policies that kept women, whether pregnant or with the potential to become pregnant, from jobs that might endanger a developing fetus. Although this case was raised by the plaintiff, the Supreme Court distinguished the decision there from that in *Echazabal*. The

Johnson Controls decision was described as "concerned with paternalistic judgments based on the broad category of gender, while the EEOC has required that judgments based on the direct threat provision be made on the basis of individualized risk assessments."

Collective Bargaining Agreements

The interplay between rights under the ADA and collective bargaining agreements was the subject of the Supreme Court's decision in *Wright v. Universal Maritime Service Corp., supra.* The Court held there that the general arbitration clause in a collective bargaining agreement does not require a plaintiff to use the arbitration procedure for an alleged violation of the ADA. However, the Court's decision was limited since the Court did not find it necessary to reach the issue of the validity of a union-negotiated waiver. In other words, the Court found that a general arbitration agreement in a collective bargaining agreement is not sufficient to waive rights under civil rights statutes but situations where there is a specific waiver of ADA rights were not addressed.[70]

Reasonable Accommodations and Seniority Systems

The Supreme Court in *U.S. Airways v. Barnett*[71] held that an employer's showing that a requested accommodation by an employee with a disability conflicts with the rules of a seniority system is ordinarily sufficient to establish that the requested accommodation is not "reasonable" within the meaning of the ADA. The Court, in a majority opinion by Justice Breyer, observed that a seniority system, "provides important employee benefits by creating, and fulfilling, employee expectations of fair, uniform treatment" and that to require a "typical employer to show more than the existence of a seniority system might undermine the employees' expectations of consistent, uniform treatment." Thus, in most ADA cases, the existence of a seniority system would entitle an employer to summary judgment in its favor. The Court found no language in the ADA which would change this presumption if the seniority system was imposed by management and not by collective bargaining. However, Justice Breyer found that there were some exceptions to this rule for "special circumstances" and gave as examples situations where (1) the employer "fairly frequently" changes the seniority system unilaterally, and thereby diminishes employee expectations to the point where one more departure would "not likely make a difference" or (2) the seniority system contains so many exceptions that one more exception is unlikely to matter.

Although the majority in *Barnett* garnered five votes, the Court's views were splintered. There were strong dissents and two concurring opinions. In her concurrence, Justice O'Connor stated that she would prefer to say that the effect of a seniority system on the ADA depends on whether the seniority system is legally enforceable but that since the result would be the same in most cases as under the majority's reasoning, she joined with the majority to prevent a stalemate. The dissents took vigorous exception to the majority's decision with Justice Scalia, joined by Justice Thomas, arguing that the ADA does not permit any seniority system to be overridden. The dissent by Justice Souter, joined by Justice Ginsberg, argued that nothing in the ADA insulated seniority rules from a reasonable accommodation requirement and that the legislative history of the ADA clearly indicated congressional intent that seniority systems be a factor in reasonable accommodations determinations but not the major factor.

Rehiring of Individual Who Has Been Terminated for Illegal Drug Use

In *Raytheon Co. v. Hernandez*,[72] the Supreme Court was presented with the issue of whether the ADA confers preferential rehiring rights on employees who have been lawfully terminated for misconduct, in this case illegal drug use. However, the Court, in an opinion by Justice Thomas, did not reach this issue, finding that the Ninth Circuit had improperly applied a disparate impact analysis in a disparate treatment case and remanding the case. The Court observed that it "has consistently recognized a distinction between claims of discrimination based on disparate treatment and claims of discrimination based on disparate impact." Disparate treatment was described as when an employer intentionally treats some people less favorably than others because of a protected characteristic such as race and liability depends on whether the protected trait actually motivated the employer's decision. Disparate impact, in contrast, involves practices that are facially neutral but in fact impact a protected group more harshly and cannot be justified by business necessity. Disparate impact cases do not require evidence of an employer's subjective intent.[73]

Employment Inquiries Relating to a Disability

Before an offer of employment is made, an employer may not ask a disability related question or require a medical examination.[74] The EEOC in its guidance on this issue stated that the rationale for this exclusion was to isolate an employer's consideration of an applicant's non-medical qualifications from any consideration of the applicant's medical condition.[75] Once an offer is made, disability related questions and medical examinations are permitted as long as all individuals who have been offered a job in that category are asked the same questions and given the same examinations.[76] It is not always clear exactly what is a medical test. In *Karraker v. Renta-Center, Inc.*,[77] the Seventh Circuit examined the issue of whether an employer's use of the Minnesota Multiphasic Personality Inventory (MMPI) in order to obtain a promotion violated the ADA. The MMPI contains questions such as "I commonly hear voices without knowing where they are coming from" and "I see things or animals or people around me that others do not see." The court found that, even though the test was not interpreted by a psychologist, the MMPI was a medical test since it was designed in part to reveal mental illness.

The events of September 11, 2001, raised questions concerning whether an employer may ask employees whether they will require assistance in the event of an evacuation because of a disability or medical condition. The EEOC issued a fact sheet stating that employers are allowed to ask employees to self-identify if they will require assistance because of a disability or medical conditions and providing details on how the employer may identify individuals who may require assistance.[78] Similarly, the 2009 H1N1 influenza pandemic also raised issues concerning inquiries relating to a disability, and the EEOC has issued guidance for employers.[79]

Defenses to a Charge of Discrimination

The ADA specifically lists defenses to a charge of discrimination, including (1) that the alleged application of qualification standards has been shown to be job related and consistent with business necessity and such performance cannot be accomplished by reasonable accommodation; (2) that the term "qualification standards" can include a requirement that an individual shall not pose a direct threat to the health or safety of other individuals in the workplace;[80] (3) that a covered entity may not use qualification standards, employment tests, or other selection criteria based on an individual's uncorrected vision unless the standard, test or selection criteria is shown to be job-related for the position in question and consistent with business necessity;[81] and (4) that religious entities may give a preference in employment to individuals of a particular religion to perform work connected with carrying on the entities' activities.[82] In addition, religious entities may require that all applicants and employees conform to the religious tenets of the organization.

The Secretary of Health and Human Services has, pursuant to a statutory requirement,[83] listed infectious diseases transmitted through the handling of food; and if the risk cannot be eliminated by reasonable accommodation, a covered entity may refuse to assign or continue to assign an individual with such a disease to a job involving food handling. [84]

Drugs, Alcohol, and Employer Conduct Rules

A controversial issue that arose during the enactment of the ADA regarding employment concerned the application of the act to drug addicts and alcoholics. The ADA provides that, with regard to employment, *current* illegal drug users are not considered to be qualified individuals with disabilities. However, former drug users and alcoholics would be covered by the act if they are able to perform the essential functions of the job. Exactly what is "current" use of illegal drugs has been the subject of some discussion. The EEOC has defined current to mean that the illegal drug use occurred "recently enough" to justify an employer's reasonable belief that drug use is an ongoing problem. [85] The courts that have examined this issue have generally found that to be covered by the ADA, the individual must be free of drugs for a considerable period of time, certainly longer than weeks.[86]

In the appendix to its regulations, EEOC further notes that "an employer, such as a law enforcement agency, may also be able to impose a qualification standard that excludes individuals with a history of illegal use of drugs if it can show that the standard is job-related and consistent with business necessity."[87] Title I of the ADA also provides that a covered entity may prohibit the illegal use of drugs and the use of alcohol in the workplace.[88] Similarly, employers may hold all employees, regardless of whether or not they have a disability, to the same performance and conduct standards.[89] However, if the misconduct results from a disability, the employer must be able to demonstrate that the rule is job-related and consistent with business necessity.[90]

Remedies

The remedies and procedures set forth in Sections 705, 706, 707, 709, and 710 of the Civil Rights Act of 1964,[91] are incorporated by reference. This provides for certain administrative enforcement as well as allowing for individual suits. The Civil Rights Act of 1991, P.L. 102-166, expanded the remedies of injunctive relief and back pay. A plaintiff who was the subject of unlawful intentional discrimination (as opposed to an employment practice that is discriminatory because of its disparate impact) may recover compensatory and punitive damages. In order to receive punitive damages, the plaintiff must show that there was a discriminatory practice engaged in with malice or with reckless indifference to the rights of the aggrieved individuals. The amount that can be awarded in punitive and compensatory damages is capped, with the amounts varying from $50,000 to $300,000 depending upon the size of the business.[92] Similarly, there is also a "good faith" exception to the award of damages with regard to reasonable accommodation.

The Lilly Ledbetter Fair Pay Act of 2009, P.L. 111-2, amends Title VII of the Civil Rights Act of 1964, the Age Discrimination in Employment Act, the Rehabilitation Act of 1973, and the Americans with Disabilities Act. Enacted in response to the Supreme Court's decision in *Ledbetter v. Goodyear Tire & Rubber Co.,*[93] the law states that an unlawful employment practice occurs, with respect to discrimination in compensation, when a discriminatory compensation decision or other practice is adopted, when an individual becomes subject to a discriminatory compensation decision or practice, or when an individual is affected by application of a discriminatory compensation decision or practice. Liability for these discriminatory practices may accrue and an individual may obtain back pay for up to two years preceding the filing of the charges.[94] P.L. 111-2 applies to Title I of the ADA which covers employment, and Section 503, 42 U.S.C. § 12203, of the ADA, which prohibits retaliation and coercion.

It should also be noted that the Supreme Court addressed the issue of punitive damages in a Title VII sex discrimination case, *Kolstad v. American Dental Association.*[95] The Court held in *Kolstad* that plaintiffs are not required to prove egregious conduct to be awarded punitive damages; however, the effect of this holding is limited by the Court's determination that certain steps taken by an employer may immunize them from punitive damages. Since the ADA incorporates the Title VII provisions, the holding in *Kolstad* may be applicable to ADA employment cases as well.[96]

In *Equal Employment Opportunity Commission v. Wal-mart Stores, Inc.,*[97] the Tenth Circuit applied *Kolstad* and affirmed an award of punitive damages under the ADA. This case involved a hearing impaired employee of Wal-mart who sometimes required the assistance of an interpreter. After being employed for about two years in the receiving department, the employee was required to attend a training session but left when the video tape shown was not close captioned and no interpreter was provided. After refusing to attend in the absence of an interpreter, the employee was transferred to the maintenance department to perform janitorial duties. When he questioned the transfer and asked for an interpreter, he was again denied. After threatening to file a complaint with the EEOC, the employee was suspended and later terminated from employment. He then sued and won compensatory damages and $75,000 in punitive damages. On appeal, the Tenth Circuit examined the reasoning in *Kolstad* and concluded that the record in *Wal-mart* "is sufficient to resolve the questions of intent and agency laid out in *Kolstad.*" With regard to intent, the court reiterated the facts and further noted that the store manager, who ultimately approved the employee's suspension, had testified that he was familiar with the ADA and its provisions regarding accommodation, discrimination and retaliation. This was seen as sufficient for a reasonable jury to conclude that Wal-mart intentionally discriminated. Wal-mart had also made an agency argument, stating that liability for punitive damages was improper because the employees who discriminated against the employee did not occupy positions of managerial control. Looking again to the reasoning in *Kolstad*, the Tenth Circuit noted that the Wal-mart employees had authority regarding hiring and firing decisions and observed that such authority is an indicium of supervisory or managerial capacity.

PUBLIC SERVICES

General Requirements

Title II of the ADA provides that no qualified individual with a disability shall be excluded from participation in or be denied the benefits of the services, programs, or activities of a public entity or be subjected to discrimination by any such entity.[98] "Public entity" is defined as state and local governments, any department or other instrumentality of a state or local government and certain transportation authorities. The ADA does not apply to the executive branch of the federal government; the executive branch and the U.S. Postal Service are covered by Section 504 of the Rehabilitation Act of 1973.[99]

The Department of Justice (DOJ) promulgated regulations for Title II which were amended as published in the Federal Register on September 15, 2010. The regulations contain a specific section on program accessibility. Each service, program, or activity conducted by a public entity, when viewed in its entirety, must be readily accessible to and usable by individuals with disabilities. However, a public entity is not required to make each of its existing facilities accessible.[100] Program accessibility is limited in certain situations involving historic preservation. In addition, in meeting the program accessibility requirement, a public entity is not required to take any action that would result in a fundamental alteration in the nature of its service, program, or activity or in undue financial and administrative burdens.[101] The amended Title II regulations adopt accessibility standards consistent with the new minimum guidelines and requirements issued by the Architectural and Transportation Barriers Compliance Board (Access Board). In order to provide "an important measure of clarity and certainty for public entities,"[102] DOJ's amended title II regulations add an "element by element safe harbor" provision where elements in covered facilities that were built or altered in accordance with the previous 1991 accessibility standards would not be required to be brought into compliance with the new standards until the elements were subject to a planned alteration. In addition, the amended regulations include more detailed standards for service animals,[103] power-driven mobility devices, ticketing, and effective communication.[104] The amended regulations took effect March 15, 2011, but compliance with the 2010 standards for accessible design is not required until March 15, 2012.

Title II of the ADA would also apply to state and local government emergency preparedness and response programs. The Department of Justice has issued an ADA guide for local governments, noting that "one of the most important roles of local government is to protect their citizenry from harm, including helping people prepare for and respond to emergencies. Making local government emergency preparedness and response programs accessible to people with disabilities is critical part of this responsibility. Making these programs accessible is also required by the ADA."[105]

Supreme Court Cases

Although Title II has not been the subject of as much litigation as Title I, several of the ADA cases to reach the Supreme Court have involved Title II. The most significant of these to date is *Tennessee v. Lane*.[106] In *Lane*, the Supreme Court held that Title II of the ADA, as it applies to the fundamental right of access to the courts, constitutes a valid exercise of congressional authority under Section 5 of the Fourteenth Amendment. In addition, the Supreme Court in *United States v. Georgia.*,[107] held that Title II of the ADA created a private cause of action for damages against the states for conduct that actually violates the Fourteenth Amendment.

In the first ADA case to reach the Supreme Court, *Pennsylvania Department of Corrections v. Yeskey, supra,* the Court found in a unanimous decision that state prisons "fall squarely within the statutory definition of 'public entity'" for Title II. *Yeskey* involved a prisoner who was sentenced to 18 to 36 months in a Pennsylvania correctional facility but was recommended for placement in a motivational boot camp for first time offenders. If the boot camp was successfully completed, the prisoner would have been eligible for parole in six months. The prisoner was denied admission to the program due to his medical history of hypertension and sued under the ADA. The state argued that state prisoners were not covered under the ADA since such coverage would "alter the usual constitutional balance between the States and the Federal Government." The Supreme Court rejected this argument, observing that "the ADA plainly covers state institutions *without* any exception that could cast the coverage of prisons into doubt." The Court noted that prisoners receive many services, including medical services, educational and vocational programs and recreational activities so that the ADA language applying the "benefits of the services, programs, or activities of a public entity" is applicable to state prisons.[108] However, the Court in *Yeskey* did not address the constitutional issues.

In *Olmstead v. Georgia, supra,* the Supreme Court examined issues raised by state mental health institutions and held that Title II of the ADA requires states to place individuals with mental disabilities in community settings rather than institutions when the State's treatment professionals have determined that community placement is appropriate, community placement is not opposed by the individual with a disability, and the placement can be reasonably accommodated.[109] "Unjustified isolation ... is properly regarded as discrimination based on disability." The *Olmstead* case had been closely watched by both disability groups and state governments. Although disability groups have applauded the holding that undue institutionalization qualifies as discrimination by reason of disability, the Supreme Court did place certain limitations on this right. In addition to the agreement of the individual affected, the Court also dealt with the issue of what is a reasonable modification of an existing program and stated: "Sensibly construed, the fundamental-alteration component of the reasonable-modifications regulation would allow the State to show that, in the allocation of available resources, immediate relief for the plaintiffs would be inequitable, given the responsibility the

State has undertaken for the care and treatment of a large and diverse population of persons with mental disabilities." This examination of what constitutes a reasonable modification may have implications for the interpretation of similar concepts in the employment and public accommodations Titles of the ADA.[110]

Other Title II Cases

Courts have examined various other issues regarding compliance with Title II. For example, in *Crowder v. Kitagawa*, a Hawaii regulation requiring the quarantine of all dogs, including guide dogs for visually impaired individuals, was found to violate Title II.[111] Other Title II cases have involved whether curb ramps are required,[112] the application of Title II to a city ordinance allowing open burning,[113] and the application of the ADA to a city's zoning ordinances.[114]

Transportation Provisions

Title II also provides specific requirements for public transportation by intercity and commuter rail and for public transportation other than by aircraft or certain rail operations.[115] All new vehicles purchased or leased by a public entity that operates a fixed route system must be accessible, and good faith efforts must be demonstrated with regard to the purchase or lease of accessible use vehicles. Retrofitting of existing buses is not required. Paratransit services must be provided by a public entity that operates a fixed route service, other than one providing solely commuter bus service.[116] Rail systems must have at least one car per train that is accessible to individuals with disabilities.[117]

Draft guidelines have been published by the Architectural and Transportation Barriers Compliance Board (Access Board) regarding the accessibility of public rights-of-way.[118] The purpose of the draft guidelines is to gather additional information for the regulatory assessment and the preparation of technical assistance materials to accompany a future rule. The Board will issue a notice of proposed rulemaking at a future date and will solicit comments at that time, prior to issuing a final rule.

Remedies

The enforcement remedies of Section 505 of the Rehabilitation Act of 1973, 29 U.S.C. §794a, are incorporated by reference.[119] These remedies are similar to those of Title VI of the Civil Rights Act of 1964, and include damages and injunctive relief. The Attorney General has promulgated regulations relating to subpart A of the Title,[120] and the Secretary of Transportation has issued regulations regarding transportation.[121]

Barnes v. Gorman

The Supreme Court in *Barnes v. Gorman*[122] held in a unanimous decision that punitive damages may not be awarded under Section 202[123] of the ADA and Section 504 of the

Rehabilitation Act of 1973.[124] Jeffrey Gorman uses a wheelchair and lacks voluntary control over his lower torso which necessitates the use of a catheter attached to a urine bag. He was arrested in 1992 after fighting with a bouncer at a nightclub and during his transport to the police station suffered significant injuries due to the manner in which he was transported. He sued the Kansas City police and was awarded over $1 million in compensatory damages and $1.2 million in punitive damages. The Eighth Circuit court of appeals upheld the award of punitive damages but the Supreme Court reversed. Although the Court was unanimous in the result, there were two concurring opinions and the concurring opinion by Justice Stevens, joined by Justices Ginsburg and Breyer, disagreed with the reasoning used in Justice Scalia's opinion for the Court.

Justice Scalia observed that the remedies for violations of both Section 202 of the ADA and Section 504 of the Rehabilitation Act are "coextensive with the remedies available in a private cause of action brought under Title VI of the Civil Rights Act of 1 964."[125] Neither Section 504 nor Title II of the ADA specifically mention punitive damages, rather they reference the remedies of Title VI of the Civil Rights Act. Title VI is based on the congressional power under the Spending Clause[126] to place conditions on grants. Justice Scalia noted that Spending Clause legislation is "much in the nature of a contract" and, in order to be a legitimate use of this power, the recipient must voluntarily and knowingly accept the terms of the "contract." "If Congress intends to impose a condition on the grant of federal moneys, it must do so unambiguously."[127] This contract law analogy was also found to be applicable to determining the scope of the damages remedies and, since punitive damages are generally not found to be available for a breach of contract, Justice Scalia found that they were not available under Title VI, Section 504 or the ADA.

PUBLIC ACCOMMODATIONS

General Requirements

Title III provides that no individual shall be discriminated against on the basis of disability in the full and equal enjoyment of the goods, services, facilities, privileges, advantages, or accommodations of any place of public accommodation by any person who owns, leases (or leases to), or operates a place of public accommodation.[128] Entities that are covered by the term "public accommodation" are listed, and include, among others, hotels, restaurants, theaters, auditoriums, laundromats, museums, parks, zoos, private schools, day care centers, professional offices of health care providers, and gymnasiums.[129] Religious institutions or entities controlled by religious institutions are not included on the list.

There are some limitations on the nondiscrimination requirements, and a failure to remove architectural barriers is not a violation unless such a removal is "readily achievable."[130] "Readily achievable" is defined as meaning "easily accomplishable and able to be carried out without much difficulty or expense."[131] Reasonable modifications in practices, policies or procedures are required unless they would fundamentally alter the nature of the goods, services, facilities, or privileges or they would result in an undue burden.[132] An undue burden is defined as an action involving "significant difficulty or expense."[133]

Title III contains a specific exemption for religious entities.[134] This applies when an entity is controlled by a religious entity. For example, a preschool that is run by a religious entity would not be covered under the ADA; however a preschool that is not run by a religious entity but that rents space from the religious entity, would be covered by Title III.

Similarly, Title III does not apply to private clubs or establishments exempted from coverage under Title II of the Civil Rights Act of 1964.[135] In interpreting this provision,[136] the Department of Justice has noted that courts have been most inclined to find private club status in cases where (1) members exercise a high degree of control over club operations, (2) the membership selection process is highly selective, (3) substantial membership fees are charged, (4) the entity is operated on a nonprofit basis, and (5) the club was not founded specifically to avoid compliance with federal civil rights law. Facilities of a private club lose their exemption, however, to the extent that they are made available for use by nonmembers as places of public accommodation.[137]

Title III also contains provisions relating to the prohibition of discrimination in public transportation services provided by private entities. Purchases of over-the-road buses are to be made in accordance with regulations issued by the Secretary of Transportation.[138]

The Department of Justice promulgated amendments to the Title III regulations that were amended as published in the *Federal Register* on September 15, 2010.[139] The amended Title III regulations adopt accessibility standards consistent with the new minimum guidelines and requirements issued by the Architectural and Transportation Barriers Compliance Board (Access Board). In addition, the regulations include more detailed standards for service animals[140] and power-driven mobility devices, ticketing, and effective communication,[141] and provide for an element by element "safe harbor" in certain circumstances. The amended regulations took effect March 15, 2011, but compliance with the 2010 standards for accessible design is not required until March 15, 2012.

Bragdon v. Abbott and Direct Threats to Health and Safety

The nondiscrimination mandate of Title III does not require that an entity permit an individual to participate in or benefit from the services of a public accommodation where such an individual poses a direct threat to the health or safety of others.[142] This issue was discussed by the Supreme Court in *Bragdon v. Abbott, supra,* where the Court stated that "the existence, or nonexistence, of a significant risk must be determined from the standpoint of the person who refuses the treatment or accommodation, and the risk assessment must be based on medical or other objective evidence." Dr. Bragdon had the duty to assess the risk of infection "based on the objective, scientific information available to him and others in his profession. His belief that a significant risk existed, even if maintained in good faith, would not relieve him from liability." The Supreme Court remanded the case for further consideration of the direct threat issue. On remand, the First Circuit Court of Appeals held that summary judgment was warranted finding that Dr. Bragdon's evidence was too speculative or too tangential to create a genuine issue of fact.[143]

The Supreme Court declined to review a Fourth Circuit Court of Appeals decision regarding the direct threat exception to Title III. In *Montalvo v. Radcliffe,*[144] the Fourth Circuit held that excluding a child who has HIV from karate classes did not violate the ADA because the child posed a significant risk to the health and safety of others which could not be eliminated by reasonable modification.

Martin v. PGA Tour and "Fundamental Alteration"

In *Martin v. PGA Tour,* the Supreme Court in a 7-2 decision by Justice Stevens held that the ADA's requirements for equal access gave a golfer with a mobility impairment the right to use a golf cart in professional competitions.[145] The Ninth Circuit had ruled that the use of the cart was permissible since it did not "fundamentally alter" the nature of the competition.[146]

Title III of the ADA defines the term "public accommodation," specifically listing golf courses.[147] The majority opinion looked at this definition and the general intent of the ADA to find that golf tours and their qualifying rounds "fit comfortably within the coverage of Title III." The Court then discussed whether there was a violation of the substantive nondiscrimination provision of Title III. The ADA states that discrimination includes "a failure to make reasonable modifications in policies, practices, or procedures, when such modifications are necessary to afford such goods, services, facilities, privileges, advantages, or accommodations to individuals with disabilities, unless the entity can demonstrate that making such modifications would fundamentally alter the nature of such goods, services, facilities, privileges, advantages, or accommodations."[148]

In theory, the Court opined, there might be a fundamental alteration of a golf tournament in two ways: (1) an alteration in an essential aspect of the game, such as changing the diameter of the hole, might be unacceptable even if it affected all players equally, or (2) a less significant change that has only a peripheral impact on the game might give a golfer with a disability an advantage over others and therefore fundamentally alter the rules of competition. Looking at both these types of situations, Justice Stevens found that a waiver of the walking rule for Casey Martin did not amount to a fundamental alteration. He noted that the essence of the game was shot-making and that the walking rule was not an indispensable feature of tournament golf as golf carts are allowed on the Senior PGA Tour as well as certain qualifying events. In addition, Justice Stevens found that the fatigue from walking the approximately five miles over five hours was not significant. Regarding the question of whether allowing Casey Martin to use a cart would give him an advantage, the majority observed that an individualized inquiry must be made concerning whether a specific modification for a particular person's disability would be reasonable under the circumstances and yet not be a fundamental alteration. In examining the situation presented, the majority found that Casey Martin endured greater fatigue even with a cart than other contenders do by walking.

Justice Scalia, joined by Justice Thomas, wrote a scathing dissent describing the majority's opinion as distorting the text of Title III, the structure of the ADA, and common sense. The dissenters contended that Title III of the ADA applies only to particular places and persons and does not extend to golf tournaments. The dissent also contended that "the rules are the rules," that they are by nature arbitrary, and there is no basis for determining any of them "non-essential."

Spector v. Norwegian Cruise Line, Ltd. and the Application of the ADA to Foreign Cruise Ships

The Supreme Court in *Spector v. Norwegian Cruise Line, Ltd.* held in a decision written by Justice Kennedy that the ADA applies to companies that operate foreign cruise ships in U.S. waters.[149] Prior to this decision there had been a split in the circuits with the Eleventh Circuit holding in *Stevens v. Premier Cruises Inc.*[150] that Title III of the ADA does apply to foreign cruise ships and the Fifth Circuit in *Spector v. Norwegian Cruise Lines*[151] holding that the ADA would not be applicable since applicability would impose U.S. law on foreign nations. The Supreme Court's decision specifically held that the statute is applicable to foreign ships in the United States waters to the same extent that it is applicable to American ships in those waters. The majority concurred that cruise ships need not comply with the ADA if modifications would conflict with international legal obligations since the ADA only requires "readily achievable" accommodations. The 5-4 decision, however, was fragmented with various Justices joining for various aspects of the opinion. It is difficult, therefore, to determine exactly what type of accommodations would be required by the application of the ADA. Since the case below had been dismissed without a trial, it was remanded to determine the statutory requirements in this particular situation. The question of whether Title III requires any permanent and significant structural modifications that interfere with the international affairs of any cruise ship, foreign flag or domestic, was specifically left undecided. Justice Scalia, in his dissenting opinion, argued that the ADA should not be interpreted to apply in the absence of a clear statement from Congress.

ADA and the Internet

The ADA was enacted in 1990, prior to widespread use of the Internet, and does not specifically cover the Internet.[152] Similarly, the ADA regulations do not specifically mention the Internet. However, the Department of Justice has indicated that it believes the ADA does require Internet accessibility,[153] and has issued an advanced notice of rulemaking (ANPR) stating that it is considering revising the regulations implementing Titles II and III of the ADA to establish specific requirements for state and local governments and public accommodations to make their websites accessible to individuals with disabilities.[154] In a hearing in the 111th Congress, DOJ testified that although the ADA does not specifically mention the Internet, access to the Internet is a civil rights issue. DOJ further stated,

> the websites of entities covered by both Title II and Title III of the statute are required by law to ensure that their sites are fully accessible to individuals with disabilities. The Department is considering issuing guidance on the range of issues that arise with regard to the internet sites of private businesses that are public accommodations covered by Title III of the ADA. In so doing, the Department will solicit public comment from the broad range of parties interested in this issue.[155]

Although the ADA was amended in 2008 to respond to a series of Supreme Court decisions that had interpreted the definition of disability narrowly it did not address the issue of Internet coverage. [156] There has been no Supreme Court decision on point, and there have been few lower court judicial decisions. The lower courts that have examined the issue have split, creating some uncertainty. In addition, the use of a "nexus" approach in *National Federation of the Blind v. Target Corporation*,[157] requiring a connection between the Internet services and the physical place in order to present an actionable ADA claim, would limit the application of the ADA to on-line retailers. Despite this uncertainty, it would appear likely that the Department of Justice's position would prevail, especially in light of the ADA's broad nondiscrimination mandate.

The question of ADA coverage of internet sites will undoubtedly continue to be a closely watched issue.[158] It should be noted that this issue does not effect the requirement that federal government websites be accessible since the federal requirement is contained in a separate statute, Section 508 of the Rehabilitation Act.[159]

Vexatious Litigation

An issue which has prompted the introduction of bills in the last several Congresses involves the filing of multiple law suits by an individual with a disability based on deminimus violations and seeking money for a settlement.[160] Although these cases are seldom tried in court, *Molski v. Mandarin Touch Restaurant*[161] did result in an opinion finding that the plaintiff was a vexatious litigant who filed hundreds of law suits designed to harass and intimidate business owners into agreeing to cash settlements. The district court ordered the plaintiff to obtain the leave of the court prior to filing any other claims under the ADA. In a related suit, the California district court also found against the counsel in the *Molski* case holding that the counsel was required to seek leave of the court before filing any additional ADA claims.[162]

These two cases were upheld on appeal to the Ninth Circuit in *Molski v. Evergreen Dynasty Corp.*[163] After a detailed examination of the cases in light of standards for vexatious litigation, the Ninth Circuit noted the following:

> For the ADA to yield its promise of equal access for the disabled, it may indeed be necessary and desirable for committed individuals to bring serial litigation advancing the time when public accommodations will be compliant with the ADA. But as important as this goal is to disabled individuals and to the public, serial litigation can become vexatious when, as here, a large number of nearly-identical complaints contain factual allegations that are contrived, exaggerated, and defy common sense.[164]

Similarly, the court of appeals held that the district court was within its discretion to impose a prefiling order. The Ninth Circuit observed "[t]hat the Frankovich Group filed numerous complaints containing false factual allegations, thereby enabled Molski's vexatious litigation, provided the district court with sufficient grounds on which to base its discretionary imposition of sanctions."[165]

Other Judicial Decisions

In *Ford v. Schering-Plough Corporation*,[166] the Third Circuit found a disparity in benefits for physical and mental illnesses did not violate the ADA and found that the disability benefits at issue did not fall within Title III. The court stated "This is in keeping with the host of examples of public accommodations provided by the ADA, all of which refer to places."[167] This conclusion was found to be in keeping with judicial decisions under Title II of the Civil Rights Act of 1964, 42 U.S.C. §2000(a).

Another issue under Title III is whether franchisers are subject to the Title. In *Nef v. American Dairy Queen Corp.*, the Fifth Circuit Court of Appeals found that a franchiser with limited control over the store a franchisee runs is not covered under Title III of the ADA.[168]

Remedies

The remedies and procedures of Title II of the Civil Rights Act of 1964 are incorporated in Title III of the ADA. Title II of the Civil Rights Act has generally been interpreted to include injunctive relief, not damages. In addition, state and local governments can apply to the Attorney General to certify that state or local building codes meet or exceed the minimum accessibility requirements of the ADA. The Attorney General may bring pattern or practice suits with a maximum civil penalty of $50,000 for the first violation and $100,000 for a violation in a subsequent case. The monetary damages sought by the Attorney General do not include punitive damages. Courts may also consider an entity's "good faith" efforts in considering the amount of the civil penalty. Factors to be considered in determining good faith include whether an entity could have reasonably anticipated the need for an appropriate type of auxiliary aid to accommodate the unique needs of a particular individual with a disability. Regulations relating to public accommodations have been promulgated by the Department of Justice[169] and regulations relating to the transportation provisions of Title III have been promulgated by the Department of Transportation.[170]

TELECOMMUNICATIONS

Title IV of the ADA amends Title II of the Communications Act of 1934[171] by adding a section providing that the Federal Communications Commission shall ensure that interstate and intrastate telecommunications relay services are available, to the extent possible and in the most efficient manner, to hearing impaired and speech impaired individuals. Any television public service announcement that is produced or funded in whole or part by any agency or instrumentality of the federal government shall include closed captioning of the verbal content of the announcement. The FCC is given enforcement authority with certain exceptions.[172]

TITLE V

Statutory Provisions

Title V contains an amalgam of provisions, several of which generated considerable controversy during ADA debate. In addition, the ADA Amendments Act of 2008 contained some additions to Title V.

Section 501 concerns the relationship of the ADA to other statutes and bodies of law. Subpart (a) states that "except as otherwise provided in this act, nothing in the act shall be construed to apply a lesser standard than the standards applied under Title V of the Rehabilitation Act ... or the regulations issued by Federal agencies pursuant to such Title." Subpart (b) provides that nothing in the act shall be construed to invalidate or limit the remedies, rights, and procedures of any federal, state, or local law that provides greater or equal protection. Nothing in the act is to be construed to preclude the prohibition of or restrictions on smoking. Subpart (d) provides that the act does not require an individual with a disability to accept an accommodation which that individual chooses not to accept.[173]

Subpart (c) of Section 501 limits the application of the act with respect to the coverage of insurance; however, the subsection may not be used as a subterfuge to evade the purposes of Titles I and III. The exact parameters of insurance coverage under the ADA are somewhat uncertain. As the EEOC has stated: "the interplay between the nondiscrimination principles of the ADA and employer provided health insurance, which is predicated on the ability to make health- related distinctions, is both unique and complex."[174] The Eighth Circuit Court of Appeals in *Henderson v. Bodine Aluminum, Inc.* issued a preliminary injunction compelling the plaintiff's employer to pay for chemotherapy that required an autologous bone marrow transplant.[175] The plaintiff was diagnosed with an aggressive form of breast cancer and her oncologist recommended entry into a clinical trial that randomly assigns half of its participants to high dose chemotherapy that necessitates an autologous bone marrow transplant. Because of the possibility that the plaintiff might have the more expensive bone marrow treatment, the employer's health plan refused to precertify the placement noting that the policy covered high dose chemotherapy only for certain types of cancer, not breast cancer. The court concluded that, "if the evidence shows that a given treatment is non-experimental— that is, if it is widespread, safe, and a significant improvement on traditional therapies—and the plan provides the treatment for other conditions directly comparable to the one at issue, the denial of treatment violates the ADA."[176]

The ADA Amendments Act made several additions to Section 501. The act states that the ADA does not alter eligibility standards for benefits under state workers' compensation laws or under state or federal disability benefit programs. P.L. 110-325 also states that nothing in the act alters the provision of Section 302(b)(2)(A)(ii),[177] specifying that reasonable modifications in policies, practices, or procedures shall be required, unless an entity can demonstrate that making such modifications in policies, practices, or procedures, including academic requirements in postsecondary education, would fundamentally alter the nature of the goods, services, facilities, privileges, advantages, or accommodations involved. The Senate Statement of Managers notes that this provision was added at the request of the higher education community and "is included solely to provide assurances that the bill does not alter current law with regard to the obligations of academic institutions under the ADA, which we believe is already demonstrated in case law on this topic."[178] The Managers' Statement also noted that this provision "is unrelated to the purpose of this legislation and should be given no meaning in interpreting the definition of disability."[179]

The ADA Amendments Act specifically prohibits reverse discrimination claims and states that nothing in the act shall provide the basis for a claim by a person without a disability that he or she was subject to discrimination because of a lack of a disability. The rules of construction provide that a covered entity under Title I, a public entity under Title II, or a person who operates a place of public accommodation under Title III, need not provide a reasonable accommodation or a reasonable modification to policies, practices, or procedures to an individual who meets the definition of disability solely under the "regarded as" prong of the definition.

Section 502 abrogates the Eleventh Amendment state immunity from suit and was discussed previously. Section 503 prohibits retaliation and coercion against an individual who has opposed an act or practice made unlawful by the ADA and was amended by the Lilly Ledbetter Fair Pay Act, P.L. 111-2, to allow for increased compensation in cases of discrimination. Section 504 requires the Architectural and Transportation Barriers Compliance Board (ATBCB) to issue guidelines regarding accessibility. Section 505 provides for attorneys' fees in "any action or administrative proceeding" under the act. Section 506, added by the ADA Amendments Act, states that "[t]he authority to issue regulations granted to the Equal Employment Opportunity Commission, the Attorney General, and the Secretary of Transportation under this Act, includes the authority to issue regulations implementing the definitions contained in sections 3 and 4." Section 507 provides for technical assistance to help entities covered by the act in understanding their responsibilities. Section 508 provides for a study by the National Council on Disability regarding wilderness designations and wilderness land management practices and "reaffirms" that nothing in the Wilderness Act is to be construed as prohibiting the use of a wheelchair in a wilderness area by an individual whose disability requires the use of a wheelchair. Section 514 provides that "where appropriate and to the extent authorized by law, the use of alternative means of dispute resolution ... is encouraged.... "[180] Section 515 provides for severability of any provision of the act that is found to be unconstitutional.

The coverage of Congress was a major controversy during the House-Senate conference on the ADA. Although the original language of the ADA did provide for some coverage of the legislative branch, Congress expanded upon this in the Congressional Accountability Act, P.L. 104-1. The major area of expansion was the incorporation of remedies that were analogous to those in the ADA applicable to the private sector.[181]

Buckhannon Board and Care Home, Inc. v. West Virginia and Attorneys' Fees

Section 505 of the ADA provides for attorneys' fees in "any action or administrative proceeding" under the act. This section was the subject of a Supreme Court decision in *Buckhannon Board and Care Home, Inc., v. West Virginia Department of Human Resources.*[182] In *Buckhannon,* the Supreme Court addressed the "catalyst theory" of attorneys' fees which posits that a plaintiff is a prevailing party if the lawsuit brings about a voluntary change in the defendant's conduct. The Court rejected this theory finding that attorneys' fees are only available where there is a judicially sanctioned change in the legal relationship of the parties.

Statutes providing for the award of attorneys' fees allow courts to make the awards to the "prevailing party." The question presented in *Buckhannon* was whether the term "prevailing party" includes a party who did not secure a judgment on the merits or a court-ordered consent decree, but has nonetheless achieved the desired result because the lawsuit has brought about a voluntary change in the defendant's conduct. The Court, in an opinion by then Chief Justice Rehnquist, examined the ADA and the Fair Housing Amendments Act (FHAA)[183] and held that the term "prevailing party" cannot be interpreted in this manner, thus rejecting the concept of a "catalyst theory." Four other members of the Court, Justices O'Connor, Scalia, Kennedy, and Thomas joined with the Chief Justice while Justices Ginsburg, Stevens, Souter and Breyer dissented.

The Court first noted that in the United States parties are ordinarily required to bear their own attorneys' fees but that Congress has authorized the award of attorneys' fees in numerous statutes in addition to the ones at issue in *Buckhannon*. These fee-shifting provisions have been interpreted in the same manner and the Court noted, citing to *Hensley v. Eckerhart*,[184] that it approached the attorneys' fees provisions of the ADA and the FHAA in this manner.

Examining prior Supreme Court cases, Chief Justice Rehnquist found that a party receiving a judgment on the merits would clearly have a basis on which attorneys' fees might be awarded. Similarly, the court found that settlement agreements enforced through a consent decree may serve as the basis for an award of attorneys' fees. The catalyst theory was seen as dissimilar from these examples since "it allows an award where there is no judicially sanctioned change in the legal relationship of the parties."[185] A voluntary change, even if it accomplished what the plaintiff sought, the Court found, "lacks the necessary judicial *imprimatur* on the change."[186]

LEGISLATION RELATING TO THE ADA IN THE 112TH CONGRESS

Changes in the ADA's statutory language to address the issue of vexatious law suits have been proposed since the 106th Congress.[187] Proponents of such legislation have argued that notification requirements would help prevent the filing of suits designed to generate money for plaintiffs and law firms.[188] Those opposed to the legislation have argued that it would undermine enforcement of the ADA and that vexatious suits are best dealt with by state bar disciplinary procedures or by the courts.[189]

On March 2, 2011, Representative Hunter introduced H.R. 881, the ADA Notification Act of 2011. H.R. 881 would add provisions to the remedies and procedures of Title III of the ADA requiring a plaintiff to provide notice of an alleged violation to the defendant by registered mail. If such notice is not provided, the bill would eliminate state or federal court jurisdiction for the action.

LEGISLATION RELATING TO THE ADA IN THE 111TH CONGRESS

Legislation to require notification prior to filing a lawsuit under Title III of the ADA, H.R. 2397, was introduced in the 111th Congress. In addition, legislation concerning access for certified trainers of service animals, H.R. 4378, was also introduced.

End Notes

[1] The ADA and Section 504 of the Rehabilitation Act of 1973, however, have not been found to cover medical treatment decisions. See e.g. *Burger v. Bloomberg*, 418 F.3d 882 (8th Cir. 2005); *McElroy v. Patient Selection Committee of the Nebraska Medical Center*, 2007 U.S. Dist. LEXIS 86321 (D. Nebraska Nov. 21, 2007)(an individual with mental illness was denied a kidney transplant on medical grounds).

[2] 42 U.S.C. §12102(b)(1).

[3] For a more detailed discussion of P.L. 110-325, see CRS Report RL34691, *The ADA Amendments Act: P.L. 110-325*, by Nancy Lee Jones.

[4] The ADA cases decided by the Supreme Court are: *Bragdon v. Abbott*, 524 U.S. 624 (1998); *Pennsylvania Department of Prisons v. Yeskey*, 524 U.S. 206 (1998); *Wright v. Universal Maritime Service Corp.*, 525 U.S. 70 (1998); *Cleveland v. Policy Management Systems*, 526 U.S. 795 (1999); *Olmstead v. L.C.*, 527 U.S. 581 (1999); *Murphy v. United Parcel Service, Inc.*, 527 U.S. 516 (1999); *Sutton v. United Air Lines, Inc.*, 527 U.S. 471(1999); *Albertson's Inc. v. Kirkingburg*, 527 U.S. 555 (1999); *Garrett v. University of Alabama*, 531 U.S. 356 (2001); *PGA Tour v. Martin*, 532 U.S. 661 (2001); *Buckhannon Board and Care Home, Inc. v. West Virginia Department of Human Resources*, 532 U.S. 598 (2001); *U.S. Airways Inc. v. Barnett*, 535 U.S. 391 (2002); *Toyota Motor Manufacturing v. Williams*, 534 U.S. 184 (2002); *Chevron USA Inc. v. Echazabal*, 536 U.S. 73 (2002); *Barnes v. Gorman*, 536 U.S. 181 (2002); *Clackamas Gastroenterology Associates, P.C. v. Wells*, 538 U.S 440 (2003); *Tennessee v. Lane*, 541 U.S. 509 (2004); *Raytheon Co. v. Hernandez*, 540 U.S. 44 (2003); *Spector v. Norwegian Cruise Line, Ltd.*, 545 U.S. 119 (2005); and *United States v. Georgia*, 546 U.S. 151 (2006). For a discussion limited to Supreme Court decisions on the ADA, see CRS Report RL31401, *The Americans with Disabilities Act: Supreme Court Decisions*, by Nancy Lee Jones.

[5] 546 U.S. 151 (2006).

[6] *Arbaugh v. Y.& H. Corp.*, 546 U.S. 500 (2006).

[7] 486 F.3d 480 (8th Cir. 2007), *cert. granted*, 552 U.S. 1074 (2007); *cert. dismissed*, 552 U.S. 1136 (2008).

[8] See e.g., *Smith v. Midland Brake, Inc.*, 180 F.3d 1154 (10th Cir. 1999), holding that a vacant position automatically goes to a qualified individual with a disability; *EEOC v. Humiston-Keeling, Inc.*, 227 F.3d 1024 (7th Cir. 2000), holding that an employer does not have to "turn away a superior applicant."

[9] 29 U.S.C. §794. For a more detailed discussion of Section 504, see CRS Report RL34041, *Section 504 of the Rehabilitation Act of 1973: Prohibiting Discrimination Against Individuals with Disabilities in Programs or Activities Receiving Federal Assistance*, by Nancy Lee Jones.

[10] 42 U.S.C. §12201(a).

[11] 42 U.S.C. §12206.

[12] See CRS Report RS21006, *Business Tax Provisions That Benefit Persons with Disabilities*, by Pamela J. Jackson, and CRS Report RS20555, *Additional Standard Tax Deduction for the Blind: A Description and Assessment*, by Pamela J. Jackson and Jennifer Teefy. See also GAO Report GAO-03-39, "Business Tax Incentives: Incentives to Employ Workers with Disabilities Receive Limited Use and Have an Uncertain Impact" (December 2002).

[13] The issue of whether the ADA definition of disability would cover individuals who are discriminated against due to a genetic condition is of less importance since the enactment of the Genetic Information Nondiscrimination Act of 2008 (GINA), P.L. 110-233. For a discussion of this act, see CRS Report RL34584, *The Genetic Information Nondiscrimination Act of 2008 (GINA)*, by Nancy Lee Jones and Amanda K. Sarata, and CRS Report R40116, *The Genetic Information Nondiscrimination Act of 2008: Selected Issues*, by Amanda K. Sarata.

[14] 42 U.S.C. §12102(3) as amended by P.L. 110-325, §4(a). For a more detailed discussion of these amendments, see CRS Report RL34691, *The ADA Amendments Act: P.L. 110-325*, by Nancy Lee Jones.

[15] Low vision devices are not included in the ordinary eyeglasses and contact lens exception.

[16] New 29 C.F.R. §1630.2(j)(3)(iii); 76 FED. REG. 17001 (March 25, 2011). For an analysis of the final regulations, CRS Report R41757, *The ADA Amendments Act Definition of Disability: Final EEOC Regulations* , by Nancy Lee Jones.

[17] 527 U.S. 471 (1999).

[18] 534 U.S. 184 (2004).

[19] 76 FED REG.16978 (March 25, 2011). For an analysis of the final regulations, CRS Report R41757, *The ADA Amendments Act Definition of Disability: Final EEOC Regulations* , by Nancy Lee Jones.

[20] H.Rept. 110-730, Part 2, at 16 (2008).

[21] 270 F.3d 445 (7th Cir. 2001).

[22] Title I of the ADA covers employment, Title II covers states and localities, and Title III covers places of public accommodations such as grocery stores, doctors' offices, and movie theaters.

[23] 42 U.S.C. §12210.

[24] H.Rept. 101-596, 101st Cong., 2d Sess. 64; 1990 U.S. Code Cong. & Ad. News 573.

[25] *Id.*

[26] 42 U.S.C. §12208.

[27] 42 U.S.C. §12211.

[28] 524 U.S. 624 (1998). For a more detailed discussion of this decision, see CRS Report 98-599, *The Americans with Disabilities Act: HIV Infection is Covered Under the Act*, by Nancy Lee Jones.

[29] 527 U.S. 471 (1999). *Toyota Motor Manufacturing v. Williams*, 534 U.S. 184 (2004).

[30] 527 U.S. 516 (1999).

[31] 527 U.S. 555 (1999).

[32] 534 U.S. 184 (2002).

[33] 524 U.S. 624 (1998).

[34] Another major issue addressed in *Bragdon* involved the interpretation of the ADA's direct threat exemption which will be discussed in the section on public accommodations. For a more detailed discussion of *Bragdon*, see CRS Report 98-599, *The Americans with Disabilities Act: HIV Infection is Covered Under the Act*, by Nancy Lee Jones.

[35] 527 U.S. 666 (1999) (The Trademark Remedy Clarification Act, TRCA, which subjected states to suit for false and misleading advertising, did not validly abrogate state sovereign immunity; neither the right to be free from a business competitor's false advertising nor a more generalized right to be secure in one's business interests qualifies as a property right protected by the Due Process Clause).

[36] 527 U.S. 627 (1999)(Congress may abrogate state sovereign immunity but must do so through legislation that is appropriate within the meaning of Section 5 of the Fourteenth Amendment; Congress must identify conduct that violates the Fourteenth Amendment and must tailor its legislation to remedying or preventing such conduct).

[37] 528 U.S. 62 (2000).

[38] 42 U.S.C. §12101(b)(4). The Commerce Clause would not be sufficient authority on which to abrogate state sovereign immunity since the Supreme Court's decision in *Seminole Tribe of Florida v. Florida*, 517 U.S. 44 (1996).

[39] 42 U.S.C. §12202.

[40] It should be noted that the Eleventh Amendment applies only to states, not municipalities. See e.g., *Ability Center of Greater Toledo v. City of Sandusky*, 385 F.3d 901 (6th Cir. 2004).

[41] 546 U.S. 151 (2006).

[42] 42 U.S.C. §12112(a), as amended by P.L. 110-325, §5. The ADA Amendments Act strikes the prohibition of discrimination against a qualified individual with a disability because of the disability of such individual and substitutes the prohibition of discrimination against a qualified individual "on the basis of disability." The Senate Managers' Statement noted that this change "ensures that the emphasis in questions of disability discrimination is properly on the critical inquiry of whether a qualified person has been discriminated against on the basis of disability, and not unduly focused on the preliminary question of whether a particular person is a 'person with a disability.'" 153 CONG. REC. S .8347 (September 11, 2008)(Statement of Managers to Accompany S. 3406, the Americans with Disabilities Act Amendments Act of 2008). Two courts of appeal have held that the prohibition of discrimination in the "terms, conditions, or privileges of employment" creates a viable cause of action for disability-based harassment. See *Flowers v. Southern Reg'l Physician Servs, Inc.*, 247 F.3d 229 (5th Cir. 2001); *Fox v. General Motors Corp.*, 247 F.3d 169 (4th Cir. 2001); *Shaver v. Independent Stave Co.*, 350 F.3d 716 (8th Cir. 2003).

[43] 42 U.S.C. §12111(5).

[44] *Arbaugh v. Y. & H. Corp.*, 546 U.S. 500 (2006).

[45] 42 U.S.C. §2000e(b).

[46] P.L. 102-166 added this provision.

[47] 42 U.S.C. §1211(8). The EEOC has stated that a function may be essential because (1) the position exists to perform the duty, (2) there are a limited number of employees available who could perform the function, or (3) the function is highly specialized. 29 C.F.R. §1630(n)(2). A number of issues have been litigated concerning essential functions. For example, some courts have found that regular attendance is an essential function of most jobs. See e.g., *Carr v. Reno*, 23 F.3d 525 (D.C.Cir. 1994), *Brenneman v. Medcentral Health System*, 366 F.3d 412 (6th Cir. 2004), *cert. denied*, 543 U.S. 1114 (2005)("the record is replete with evidence of plaintiff's excessive absenteeism, which rendered him unqualified for that position.") In *Mulloy v. Acushnet Co.*, 460 F.3d 141 (1st Cir. 2006), the first circuit found that an essential function of the job at issue included being physically present at the plant in order to perform troubleshooting and take corrective actions and found that the plaintiff could not perform the job's essential functions remotely. In *Fraizier v. Simmons*, 254 F.3d 1247 (10th Cir. 2001), the tenth circuit held that a crime investigator with MS was not otherwise qualified to perform his job duties since it would be very difficult for him to stand or walk for prolonged periods, to run or to physically restrain persons. Similarly, a nurse with a back injury that prevented her from lifting more than 15 or 20 pounds was not a qualified individual with a disability since the ability to lift fifty pounds was an essential function of her job. *Phelps v. Optima Health, Inc.*, 251 F.3d 21 (1st Cir. 2001).

[48] See 45 C.F.R. Part 84.

[49] 42 U.S.C. § 12111(9).

[50] 42 U.S.C. §12111(10).

[51] EEOC, "EEOC Enforcement Guidance on Reasonable Accommodation and Undue Hardship Under the Americans with Disabilities Act," No. 915.002 (March 1, 1999).

[52] http://www.eeoc.gov/policy/docs/accommodation.html#requesting.

[53] It should be emphasized that the EEOC's guidance does not have the force of regulations and courts are not bound to follow the guidance although some courts do defer to agency expertise.

[54] 29 C.F.R. §1630.9.

[55] http://www.eeoc.gov/policy/docs/accommodation.html.

[56] 44 F.3d 538 (7th Cir. 1995).

[57] *Id.* At 542-543. See also *Schmidt v. Methodist Hospital of Indiana*, 89 F.3d 342 (7th Cir. 1996), where the court found that reasonable accommodation does not require an employer to provide everything an employee requests.

[58] 538 U.S. 440 (2003).

[59] 42 U.S.C. §12111(4).

[60] EEOC Compliance Manual §605:0009.

[61] 426 F.3d 887 (7th Cir. 2005).

[62] *Id.* at 892.

[63] 527 U.S. 555 (1999).

[64] 536 U.S. 73 (2002).

[65] 42 U.S.C. §12113(a).

[66] 42 U.S.C. §12113(b).

[67] 226 F.3d 1063 (9th Cir. 2000).

[68] 29 C.F.R. §1630.15(b)(2).

[69] 499 U.S. 187 (1991).

[70] For more information, see CRS Report RL30008, *Labor and Mandatory Arbitration Agreements: Background and Discussion*, by Jon O. Shimabukuro.

[71] 535 U.S. 391 (2002).

[72] 540 U.S. 44 (2003).

[73] Upon review, the Ninth Circuit Court of Appeals reversed and remanded the district court's grant of the employer's motion for summary judgment. *Hernandez v. Hughes Missile Systems Co.*, 362 F.3d 564 (9th Cir. 2004).

[74] 42 U.S.C. §12112.

[75] EEOC, "ADA Enforcement Guidance: Preemployment Disability-Related Questions and Medical Examinations," October 10, 1995.

[76] *Id.*

[77] 411 F.3d 831 (7th Cir. 2005). For a more detailed discussion of this case, see Maureen E. Mulvihill, "*Karraker v. Rent-a-Center:* Testing the Limits of the ADA, Personality Tests, and Employer Preemployment Screening," 37 LOY. U. CHI. L. J. 865 (2006).

[78] http://www.eeoc.gov/facts/evacuation. For a detailed discussion of emergency procedures for employees with disabilities, see Federal Emergency Management Agency, "Emergency Procedures for Employees with Disabilities in Office Occupancies." http://www.securitymanagement.com/library/disable.html.

[79] See http://www.eeoc.gov/facts/pandemic_flu.html. For a discussion of these issues, see CRS Report R40866, *The Americans with Disabilities Act (ADA): Employment Issues and the 2009 Influenza Pandemic*, by Nancy Lee Jones.

[80] The EEOC in its regulations states that the following factors should be considered when determining whether an individual poses a direct threat: the duration of the risk, the nature and severity of the potential harm, the likelihood that the potential harm will occur, and the imminence of the potential harm. 29 C.F.R. § 163 0.2(r).

[81] This provision was added by P.L. 110-325, §5.

[82] 42 U.S.C. § 12113.

[83] *Id.*

[84] 62 F.R. 49518 (September 22, 1997).

[85] 29 C.F.R. Appendix §1630.3.

[86] See e.g., *Shafer v. Preston Memorial Hospital Corp.*, 107 F.3d 274 (4th Cir. 1997)(individual is a current user if he or she has illegally used drugs "in a periodic fashion during the weeks and months prior to discharge.")

[87] 29 C.F.R. Appendix §1630.3.

[88] 42 U.S.C. §12114(c); 29 C.F.R. §1630. 16(b)(4).

[89] EEOC Compliance Manual §902.2(c)(4). See also *Hamilton v. Southwestern Bell Telephone Co.*, 136 F.3d 1047 (5th Cir. 1998)("the ADA does not insulate emotional or violent outbursts blamed on an impairment").

[90] EEOC Enforcement Guidance on the ADA and Psychiatric Disabilities, No. 9 15.002, p. 29 (March 25, 1997).

[91] 42 U.S.C. §§2000e-4, 2000e-5, 2000e-6, 2000e-8, 2000e-9.

[92] In *Gagliardo v. Connaught Laboratories*, 311 F.3d 565 (3d Cir. 2002), an employee who claimed that she was discriminated against due to her multiple sclerosis won an award of $2.3 million despite the ADA caps. The

court found that the judge had properly proportioned the claims between the federal and state causes of action and found that the fact that the state law did not contain a cap indicated that it was intended to provide a remedy beyond the federal remedies.

[93] 550 U.S. 618 (2007).

[94] For a discussion of the *Ledbetter* decision, see CRS Report RS22686, *Pay Discrimination Claims Under Title VII of the Civil Rights Act: A Legal Analysis of the Supreme Court's Decision in Ledbetter v. Goodyear Tire & Rubber Co., Inc.*, by Jody Feder. For a discussion of the legislation, see CRS Report RL3 1867, *Pay Equity Legislation*, by Jody Feder.

[95] 527 U.S. 526 (1999).

[96] But see *Barnes v. Gorman*, 536 U.S. 181 (2002), where the Supreme Court held that punitive damages may not be awarded under Section 202 of the ADA.

[97] 187 F.3d 1241 (10th Cir. 1999).

[98] 42 U.S.C. §§12131-12133.

[99] 29 U.S.C. §794.

[100] 28 C.F.R. §35.150.

[101] *Id.* The Department of Justice provided a document containing examples of common ADA compliance problems by city governments that have been identified through the Department of Justice's ongoing enforcement efforts. See http://www.usdoj.gov/crt/ada/comprob.htm.

[102] 75 FED. REG. 56207 (September 15, 2010). The Department of Justice amended existing Title II and Title III regulations. For a more detailed discussion of the safe harbor provision see CRS Report R41376, *The Americans with Disabilities Act (ADA): Final Rule Amending Title II and Title III Regulations*, by Nancy Lee Jones.

[103] For a more detailed discussion of the provisions relating to service animals see CRS Report R41468, *The Americans with Disabilities Act (ADA) and Service Animals*, by Nancy Lee Jones.

[104] 75 FED. REG. 56164 (September 15, 2010). For a more detailed discussion of the changes generally see CRS Report R41376, *The Americans with Disabilities Act (ADA): Final Rule Amending Title II and Title III Regulations*, by Nancy Lee Jones.

[105] http://www.usdoj.gov/crt/ada/emergencyprep.htm. For a more detailed discussion of these issues, see CRS Report RS22254, *The Americans with Disabilities Act and Emergency Preparedness and Response*, by Nancy Lee Jones.

[106] 541 U.S. 509 (2004).

[107] 546 U.S. 151 (2006).

[108] The Supreme Court had remanded this case for consideration of whether Yeskey was an individual with a disability. On remand, the district court held that he was not covered by the ADA since he was not substantially limited in a major life activity. *Yeskey v. Pennsylvania Department of Corrections*, 76 F.Supp. 2d 572 (M.D. Pa. 1999).

[109] *Olmstead* has focused federal and state attention on the development of policies that would expand home and community-based care for individuals with disabilities. For a more detailed discussion of *Olmstead*, see CRS Report R40 106, *Olmstead v. L. C.: Judicial and Legislative Developments in the Law of Deinstitutionalization*, by Emily C. Barbour.

[110] See also *Frederick L., Nina S., Kevin C. And Steven F. v. Department of Public Welfare*, 422 F.3d 151 (3d Cir. 2005), where the court found that Pennsylvania's Department of Public Welfare was obligated to integrate eligible patients into local community-based settings and was required to articulate a commitment to this requirement in a specific comprehensive, effectively working, plan before it could utilize a "fundamental alteration" defense.

[111] *Crowder v. Kitagawa*, 81 F.3d 1480 (9th Cir. 1996). The court stated: "Although Hawaii's quarantine requirement applies equally to all persons entering the state with a dog, its enforcement burdens visually-impaired persons in a manner different and greater than it burdens others. Because of the unique dependence upon guide dogs among many of the visually-impaired, Hawaii's quarantine effectively denies these persons ... meaningful access to state services, programs, and activities while such services, programs, and activities remain open and easily accessible by others."

[112] In *Kinney v. Yerusalim*, 812 F.Supp. 547 (E.D. Pa. 1993), *aff'd* 9 F.3d 1067 (3d Cir. 1993), *cert. denied*, 511 U.S. 1033 (1994), the court found that street repair projects must include curb ramps for individuals with disabilities. Similarly, see *Ability Center of Greater Toledo v. Lechner*, 385 F.3d 901 (6th Cir. 2004), where the court held that Title II "does not merely prohibit intentional discrimination. It also imposes on public entities the requirement that they provide qualified disabled individuals with meaningful access to public services, which in certain instances necessitates that public entities take affirmative steps to remove architectural barriers to such access in the process of altering existing facilities." At 912. See also *Barden v. Sacramento*, 292 F.3d 1073 (9th Cir. 2002), *cert. denied*, 539 U.S. 958 (2003). See also 28 C.F.R. §35.151(e)(1), where the Department of Justice details the requirements for curb ramps.

[113] *Heather K. v. City of Mallard, Iowa*, 946 F.Supp. 1373 (N.D.Iowa 1996).

[114] *Innovative Health Systems, Inc. v. City of White Plains*, 117 F.3d 37 (2d Cir. 1997).

[115] 42 U.S.C. §§12141-12165. P.L. 104-287 added a new definition. The term "commuter rail transportation" has the meaning given the term "commuter rail passenger transportation" in 45 U.S.C. §502(9). For a more detailed discussion of the transportation provisions, see CRS Report RS22676, *Public Transportation Providers' Obligations Under the Americans with Disabilities Act (ADA)*, by Emily C. Barbour. Airplanes are covered by the Air Carriers Access Act, 49 U.S.C. § 41705. For a discussion of this law, see CRS Report RL34047, *Overview of the Air Carrier Access Act (ACAA)*, by Emily C. Barbour.

[116] 42 U.S.C. §12143.

[117] 42 U.S.C. § 12162.

[118] 70 Fed. Reg. 70734 (November 23, 2005).

[119] 42 U.S.C. §12133.

[120] 28 C.F.R. Part 35.

[121] 49 C.F.R. Parts 27, 37, 38.

[122] 536 U.S. 181 (2002).

[123] 42 U.S.C. §12132. Section 203, 42 U.S.C. §12133, contains the enforcement provisions.

[124] 29 U.S.C. §794. Section 504 in relevant part prohibits discrimination against individuals with disabilities in any program or activity that receives federal financial assistance. The requirements of Section 504, its regulations, and judicial decisions were the model for the statutory language in the ADA where the nondiscrimination provisions are not limited to entities that receive federal financial assistance.

[125] 42 U.S.C. §2000d *et seq.*

[126] U.S. Const., Art. I §8, cl.1.

[127] *Pennhurst State School and Hospital v. Halderman*, 451 U.S. 1, 17 (1981).

[128] 42 U.S.C. §12182.

[129] 42 U.S.C. §12181.

[130] 42 U.S.C. §12182(b)(2)(A)(iv).

[131] 42 U.S.C. §12181.

[132] 42 U.S.C. §12182(b)(2)(A).

[133] 28 C.F.R. §36.104.

[134] 42 U.S.C. §12187.

[135] 42 U.S.C. §2000a-3(a).

[136] 42 U.S.C. 12187.

[137] Department of Justice, "ADA Title III Technical Assistance Manual" III-1.6000.

[138] 42 U.S.C. § 12184. This section was amended by P.L. 104-59 to provide that accessibility requirements for private over-the-road buses must be met by small providers within three years after the issuance of final regulations and with respect to other providers, within two years after the issuance of such regulations.

[139] 75 FED. REG. 56164 (September 15, 2010). For a more detailed discussion of the changes generally see CRS Report R41376, *The Americans with Disabilities Act (ADA): Final Rule Amending Title II and Title III Regulations*, by Nancy Lee Jones.

[140] For a more detailed discussion of the provisions relating to service animals see CRS Report R41468, *The Americans with Disabilities Act (ADA) and Service Animals*, by Nancy Lee Jones.

[141] For a more detailed discussion the amended regulations regarding effective communication in the hospital setting see CRS Report 97-826, *Americans with Disabilities Act (ADA) Requirements Concerning the Provision of Interpreters by Hospitals and Doctors*, by Nancy Lee Jones. For a discussion of an advanced notice of proposed rulemaking (ANPR) regarding captioning see CRS Report R41659, *The Americans with Disabilities Act (ADA): Movie Captioning and Video Description*, by Nancy Lee Jones.

[142] For a more detailed discussion of this issue, see CRS Report RS22219, *The Americans with Disabilities Act (ADA) Coverage of Contagious Diseases*, by Nancy Lee Jones. The EEOC has discussed the concept of direct threat in the context of an influenza pandemic and determined that "[w]hether pandemic influenza rises to the level of a direct threat depends on the severity of the illness." http://www.eeoc.gov/facts/pandemic_flu.html.

[143] *Abbott v. Bragdon*, 163 F.3d 87 (1st Cir. 1998), *cert. denied*, 526 U.S. 1131 (1999).

[144] 167 F.3d 873 (4th Cir. 1999), *cert. denied*, 528 U.S. 813 (1999).

[145] 532 U.S. 661 (2001).

[146] 204 F.3d 994 (9th Cir. 2000).

[147] 42 U.S.C. §12181(7).

[148] 42 U.S.C. §12182(b)(2)(A)(ii)(emphasis added). The Department of Justice regulations echo the statutory language and provide the following illustration. "A health care provider may refer an individual with a disability to another provider if that individual is seeking, or requires, treatment or services outside of the referring provider's area of specialization, and if the referring provider would make a similar referral for an individual without a disability who seeks or requires the same treatment or services." 28 C.F.R. §36.302. The concept of fundamental alteration did not originate in the statutory language of the ADA but was derived from Supreme Court interpretation of Section 504 of the Rehabilitation Act of 1973, 29 U.S.C. §794, which, in part, prohibits discrimination against an individual with a disability in any program or activity that receives federal financial assistance and was the model on which the ADA was based. In *Southeastern Community College v.*

Davis, 442 U.S. 397 (1979), the Supreme Court addressed a suit by a hearing impaired woman who wished to attend a college nursing program. The college rejected her application because it believed her hearing disability made it impossible for her to participate safely in the normal clinical training program and to provide safe patient care. The Supreme Court found no violation of Section 504 and held that it did "not encompass the kind of curricular changes that would be necessary to accommodate respondent in the nursing program." Since Davis could not function in clinical courses without close supervision, the Court noted that the college would have had to limit her to academic courses. The Court further observed that "whatever benefits respondent might realize from such a course of study, she would not receive even a rough equivalent of the training a nursing program normally gives. Such a fundamental alteration in the nature of a program is far more than the 'modification' the regulation requires." (At 409-410.) In conclusion, the Court found that "nothing in the language or history of § 504 reflects an intention to limit the freedom of an educational institution to require reasonable physical qualifications for admission to a clinical training program." (At 414.)

[149] 545 U.S. 119 (2005).

[150] 215 F.3d 1237 (11th Cir. 2000), rehearing and rehearing en banc denied, 284 F.3d 1187 (11th Cir. 2002).

[151] 356 F.3d 641 (5th Cir. 2004).

[152] For a more detailed discussion of this issue, see CRS Report R40462, *The Americans with Disabilities Act: Application to the Internet*, by Nancy Lee Jones. A similar issue is raised by electronic book readers. See http://www.ada.gov/kindle_ltr_eddoj.htm.

[153] *Achieving the Promise of the Americans with Disabilities Act in the Digital Age: Current Issues, Challenges, and Opportunities: Hearing Before the H. Subcommittee on the Constitution, Civil Rights and Civil Liberties of the H. Comm. on the Judiciary*, 111th Cong., 2d Sess. (Testimony of Samuel R. Bagenstos, Principal Deputy Assistant Attorney General for Civil Rights, Department of Justice), http://judiciaryBagenstos100422.pdf.

[154] http://www.ada.gov/anprm2010/web

[155] *Id.*

[156] The ADA Amendments Act, P.L. 110-325. For a more detailed discussion of P.L. 110-325, see CRS Report RL34691, *The ADA Amendments Act: P.L. 110-325*, by Nancy Lee Jones.

[157] 452 F.Supp.2d 946 (N.D. Calif. 2006). The case was settled on August 27, 2008. See http://www.nfb.org. For a more detailed discussion of this case, see Isabel Arana DuPree, "Websites as 'Places of Public Accommodation': Amending the Americans with Disabilities Act in the Wake of *National Federal of the Blind v. Target Corporation*," NC J. L. & Tech. 273 (2007); Jeffrey Bashaw, "Applying the Americans with Disabilities Act to Private Websites after *National Federation of the Blind v. Target*," 4 Shidler J. L. Com. & Tech. 3 (2008).

[158] For a more detailed discussion of the issue, see National Council on Disability, "When the Americans with Disabilities Act Goes Online: Application of the ADA to the Internet and the Worldwide Web," (July 10, 2003) http://www.ncd.gov/newsroom/publications/2003/adainternet.htm; The Association of the Bar of the City of New York, "Website Accessibility for People with Disabilities," 62 The Record 118 (2007); Steven Mendelsohn, and Martin Gould, "When the Americans with Disabilities Act Goes Online: Application of the ADA to the Internet and the World Wide Web," 7 Comp. L. Rev. & Tech. J. 173 (2004).

[159] 29 U.S.C. §794(d), as amended by P.L. 105-220. Section 508 requires that the electronic and information technology used by federal agencies be accessible to individuals with disabilities, including employees and member of the public. Generally, Section 508 requires each federal department or agency and the U.S. Postal Service to ensure that individuals with disabilities who are federal employees have access to and use of electronic and information technology that is comparable to that of individuals who do not have disabilities. For more detailed information, see http://www.section508.gov.

[160] See section on legislation *infra*. See also CRS Report RS22296, *The Americans with Disabilities Act: Legislation Concerning Notification Prior to Initiating Legal Action*, by Nancy Lee Jones. For a discussion of vexatious lawsuits, see Wayne C. Arnold and Lisa D. Herzog, "How Many Lawsuits Does It Take to Declare an ADA Plaintiff Vexatious?" 48 Orange County Lawyer 50 (July 2006).

[161] 347 F.Supp.2d 860 (C.D.Calif. 2004).

[162] *Molski v. Mandarin Touch Restaurant*, 359 F.Supp.2d 924 (C.D.Calif. 2005).

[163] 500 F.3d 1047 (9th Cir. 2007), cert. denied, 129 S. Ct. 594, 172 L. Ed. 2d 455 (2008).

[164] *Id.* at 38.

[165] *Id.* at 43.

[166] 145 F.3d 601(3d Cir. 1998), *cert. denied*, 525 U.S. 1093 (1999).

[167] *Id.* at 612.

[168] 58 F.3d 1063 (5th Cir. 1995), *cert. denied*, 516 U.S. 1045 (1996).

[169] 28 C.F.R. Part 36.

[170] 49 C.F.R. Parts 27, 37, 38.

[171] 47 U.S.C. §§201 *et seq.*

[172] 47 U.S.C. §255. For an FCC discussion of closed captioning, see http://www.fcc.gov/cgb/consumerfacts/closedcaption.html.

[173] 29 U.S.C. §§790 *et seq.*

[174] EEOC, "Interim Policy Guidance on ADA and Health Insurance," BNA's Americans with Disabilities Act Manual 70:1051 (June 8, 1993). This guidance deals solely with the ADA implications of disability-based health insurance plan distinctions and states that "insurance distinctions that are not based on disability, and that are applied equally to all insured employees, do not discriminate on the basis of disability and so do not violate the ADA."

[175] 70 F.3d 958 (8th Cir. 1995).

[176] See also *Rogers v. Department of Health and Environmental Control*, 174 F.3d 431 (4th Cir. 1999), where the fourth circuit court of appeals held that the ADA does not require employers to offer the same long-term disability insurance benefits for mental and physical disabilities. For a more detailed discussion of the ADA and coverage of mental and physical disabilities in insurance, see Matthew G. Simon, "Not All Illnesses Are Treated Equally - Does a Disability Benefits Plan Violate the ADA by Providing Less Generous Long-Term Benefits for Mentally Disabled Employees than for Physically Disabled Employees?" 8 U. Pa. J. Lab. & Emp. L. 943 (Summer 2006).

[177] 42 U.S.C. §12182(b)(2)(A)(ii).

[178] 153 CONG. REC. S. 8347 (Sept. 11, 2008)(Statement of Managers to Accompany S. 3406) the Americans with Disabilities Act Amendments Act of 2008).

[179] *Id.*

[180] 42 U.S.C. § 12212.

[181] Congress has also applied the employment and public accommodation provisions of the ADA to the Executive Office of the President. P.L. 104-331 (October 26, 1996).

[182] 532 U.S. 598 (2001).

[183] 42 U.S.C. §3613(c)(2).

[184] 461 U.S. 424 (1983).

[185] 532 U.S. 598, 605 (2001).

[186] *Id.*

[187] For a more detailed discussion, see CRS Report RS22296, *The Americans with Disabilities Act: Legislation Concerning Notification Prior to Initiating Legal Action*, by Nancy Lee Jones; Carri Becker, "Private Enforcement of the Americans with Disabilities Act via Serial Litigation: Abusive or Commendable?," 17 Hastings Women's L.J. 93 (2006). See also the preceding discussion of judicial decisions under Title III, which have attempted to respond to the issue of vexatious litigants.

[188] See Testimony of the Honorable Mark Foley, hearing on H.R. 3590, The ADA Notification Act, Before the House Committee on the Judiciary, Subcommittee on the Constitution, May 18, 2000. Published at http://www.house.gov/ judiciary/fole05 1 8.htm.

[189] See Letter to Honorable Charles Canady, chairman, Subcommittee on the Constitution, House Committee on the Judiciary from Robert Raben, Assistant Attorney General reprinted at http://commdocs.house.gov/committees/ judiciary/hju66728.000/hju66728_0f.htm.

In: The Americans with Disabilities Act (ADA): Provisions...   ISBN: 978-1-61470-961-9
Editor: John Kiviniemi and Cécile Sanjo   © 2012 Nova Science Publishers, Inc.

Chapter 2

THE ADA AMENDMENTS ACT: P.L. 110-325

Nancy Lee Jones

SUMMARY

The Americans with Disabilities Act (ADA) is a broad civil rights act prohibiting discrimination against individuals with disabilities. As stated in the act, its purpose is "to provide a clear and comprehensive national mandate for the elimination of discrimination against individuals with disabilities."

The threshold issue in any ADA case is whether the individual alleging discrimination is an individual with a disability. Several Supreme Court decisions, including those in *Sutton v. United Air Lines, Inc.*, 527 U.S. 471 (1999), and *Toyota Motor Manufacturing v. Williams*, 534 U.S. 184 (2004), have interpreted the definition of disability, generally limiting its application. Since these Supreme Court interpretations, lower court decisions also interpreted the definition of disability strictly. Congress responded to these decisions by enacting the ADA Amendments Act, P.L. 110-325, which rejects the Supreme Court and lower court interpretations and amends the ADA to provide broader coverage. On September 23, 2009, the Equal Employment Opportunity Commission (EEOC) issued proposed regulations under the ADA Amendments Act.

INTRODUCTION

The Americans with Disabilities Act (ADA)[1] is a broad civil rights act prohibiting discrimination against individuals with disabilities. As stated in the act, its purpose is "to provide a clear and comprehensive national mandate for the elimination of discrimination against individuals with disabilities."[2]

The threshold issue in any ADA case is whether the individual alleging discrimination is an individual with a disability. Several Supreme Court decisions have interpreted the definition of disability, generally limiting its application.[3] Since these Supreme Court interpretations, lower court decisions also interpreted the definition of disability strictly.

Congress responded to these decisions by enacting the ADA Amendments Act, P.L. 110-325, which rejects the Supreme Court and lower court interpretations and amends the ADA to provide broader coverage. Two of the major changes made by the ADA Amendments Act are to expand the current interpretation of when an impairment substantially limits a major life activity (rejecting the Supreme Court's interpretation in *Toyota)*, and to require that the determination of whether an impairment substantially limits a major life activity must be made without regard to the use of mitigating measures (rejecting the Supreme Court's decisions in *Sutton, Murphy,* and *Kirkingburg)*. On September 23, 2009, the Equal Employment Opportunity Commission (EEOC) issued proposed regulations under the ADA Amendments Act. Comment on the proposed regulations must be submitted on or before November 23, 2009.[4]

BACKGROUND

The original ADA definition of disability was based on the definition of disability used for Section 504 of the Rehabilitation Act of 1973.[5] The term disability with respect to an individual was defined as "(A) a physical or mental impairment that substantially limits one or more of the major life activities of such individual; (B) a record of such an impairment; or (C) being regarded as having such an impairment."[6] The ADA Amendments Act essentially keeps the same language but rejects the interpretation given to the language by the Supreme Court.

Three Supreme Court decisions in 1999 addressed the definition of disability, and specifically discussed the concept of mitigating measures. *Sutton v. United Air Lines* involved sisters who were rejected from employment as pilots with United Air Lines because they wore eyeglasses. The Supreme Court in *Sutton* examined the definition of disability used in the original ADA and found that the determination of whether an individual has a disability should be made with reference to measures that mitigate the individual's impairment. The *Sutton* Court stated, "'a disability' exists only where an impairment 'substantially limits' a major life activity, not where it 'might,' 'could,' or 'would' be substantially limiting if mitigating measures were not taken." The Court also emphasized that the statement of findings in the ADA that some 43 million Americans have one or more physical or mental disabilities "requires the conclusion that Congress did not intend to bring under the statute's protection all those whose uncorrected conditions amount to disabilities."

Similarly, in *Murphy v. United Parcel Service, Inc.*, the Court held that the fact that an individual with high blood pressure was unable to meet the Department of Transportation (DOT) safety standards was not sufficient to create an issue of fact regarding whether an individual is regarded as unable to utilize a class of jobs. The Court in *Murphy* found that an employee is regarded as having a disability if the covered entity mistakenly believes that the employee's actual, nonlimiting impairment substantially limits one or more major life activities. And in the last of this trilogy of 1999 cases, the Court in *Kirkingburg v. Albertsons* held that a trucker with monocular vision who was able to compensate for this impairment was not a person with a disability.

In the 2002 case of *Toyota Motor Manufacturing v. Williams,* the meaning of "substantially limits" was examined, and Justice O'Connor, writing for the unanimous Court, determined that the word substantial "clearly precluded impairments that interfere in only a minor way with the performance of manual tasks." The Court also found that the term "major life activity" "refers to those activities that are of central importance to daily life." Finding that these terms are to be "interpreted strictly," the Court held that "to be substantially limited in performing manual tasks, an individual must have an impairment that prevents or severely restricts the individual from doing activities that are of central importance to most people's daily lives."

Since these Supreme Court decisions, lower courts applied these holdings in various factual situations. For example, in *Orr v. Wal-Mart Stores, Inc.*,[7] the Eighth Circuit found that a pharmacist with diabetes who takes insulin and eats a special diet was not an individual with a disability because, with the medication and diet, the diabetes did not substantially affect a major life activity. Similarly, in *McClure v. General Motors Corp.*,[8] the Fifth Circuit found that an electrician with muscular dystrophy who could lift his arms only to shoulder level did not have a disability. The Eleventh Circuit examined what are major life activities in *Littleton v. Wal-Mart*.[9] The plaintiff, a 29-year-old man who was diagnosed with mental retardation as a child, was not hired for a position as a cart-push associate with Wal-Mart. The court found that "[i]t was unclear whether thinking, communicating and social interaction are 'major life activities' under the ADA" and noted that even if thinking, communicating, and social interaction were found to be major life activities, the plaintiff did not show that he was substantially limited in these activities.[10]

THE AMERICANS WITH DISABILITIES AMENDMENTS ACT

Legislative Background

On July 26, 2007, the 17th anniversary of the enactment of the ADA, bills were introduced in both the House and Senate to amend the ADA to broaden the definition of disability.[11] S. 1881, introduced by Senator Harkin, was referred to the Senate Health, Education, Labor, and Pensions Committee and hearings were held on November 15, 2007.[12] H.R. 3195, introduced by Representative Hoyer, was referred to the House Committee on Education and Labor, as well as the House Committees on Judiciary, Transportation and Infrastructure, and Energy and Commerce for a period to be determined by the Speaker. Hearings were held by the Subcommittee on the Constitution, Civil Rights, and Civil Liberties of the House Judiciary Committee on October 4, 2007,[13] and on January 29, 2008, by the House Education and Labor Committee.[14]

On June 18, 2008, both the House Judiciary Committee and the House Education and Labor Committee reported out H.R. 3195, now renamed the ADA Amendments Act of 2008. H.R. 3195 as reported out of committee was significantly different from H.R. 3195 and S. 1881 as introduced.[15] Those bills would have eliminated the phrase "substantially limits" from the definition thereby broadening the definition of disability to cover the majority of the population. The House passed H.R. 3195 on June 25, 2008, by a vote of 402 to 17. The House-passed bill would have kept the term "substantially limits" and defined it as "materially restricts."

The Senate Health, Education, Labor and Pensions Committee held a hearing on July 15, 2008, where testimony was heard on several issues, including the impact of the ADA Amendments Act on education.[16] On July 31, 2008, Senator Harkin with 55 original cosponsors introduced S. 3406, the ADA Amendments Act of 2008, which tracked much of the House-passed language but made several significant changes, including deleting the House definition of "substantially limits" as "materially restricts." S. 3406 passed the Senate by unanimous consent on September 11, 2008,[17] and passed the House September 17, 2008. P.L. 110-325 was signed into law on September 25, 2008.

General Definition of Disability

Definition and Rules of Construction

The ADA Amendments Act (ADAAA) defines the term disability with respect to an individual as "(A) a physical or mental impairment that substantially limits one or more of the major life activities of such individual; (B) a record of such an impairment; or (C) being regarded as having such an impairment (as described in paragraph (3))."[18] Although this is essentially the same statutory language as was in the original ADA, P.L. 110-325 contains new rules of construction regarding the definition of disability, which provide that

- the definition of disability shall be construed in favor of broad coverage to the maximum extent permitted by the terms of the act;
- the term "substantially limits" shall be interpreted consistently with the findings and purposes of the ADA Amendments Act;
- an impairment that substantially limits one major life activity need not limit other major life activities to be considered a disability;
- an impairment that is episodic or in remission is a disability if it would have substantially limited a major life activity when active; and
- the determination of whether an impairment substantially limits a major life activity shall be made without regard to the ameliorative effects of mitigating measures, except that the ameliorative effects of ordinary eyeglasses or contact lenses shall be considered.[19]

The findings of the ADA Amendments Act include statements indicating that the Supreme Court decisions in *Sutton* and *Toyota* as well as lower court cases have narrowed and limited the ADA from what was intended by Congress. P.L. 110-325 specifically states that the then-current Equal Employment Opportunity Commission (EEOC) regulations defining the term "substantially limits" as "significantly restricted" are "inconsistent with congressional intent, by expressing too high a standard." The codified findings in the original ADA are also amended to delete the finding that "43,000,000 Americans have one or more physical or mental disabilities." This finding was used in *Sutton* to support limiting the reach of the definition of disability.

Substantially Limits a Major Life Activity

The ADA Amendments Act states that the purposes of the legislation are to carry out the ADA's objectives of the elimination of discrimination and the provision of "'clear, strong, consistent, enforceable standards addressing discrimination' by reinstating a broad scope of protection available under the ADA." P.L. 110-325 rejected the Supreme Court's holdings that mitigating measures are to be used in making a determination of whether an impairment substantially limits a major life activity as well as holdings defining the "substantially limits" requirements. The substantially limits requirements of *Toyota* as well as the EEOC regulations defining substantially limits as "significantly restricted" are specifically rejected in the new law. The proposed EEOC regulations state that "[a]n impairment need not prevent, or significantly or severely restrict, the individual from performing a major life activity in order to be considered a disability."[20]

The Senate Statement of Managers notes that the courts had not interpreted the term "substantially limits" in the manner Congress had intended and discussed the methods Congress had considered in order to express its intent. The House of Representatives had defined the term "substantially limits" as "materially restricts" in order "to convey that Congress intended to depart from the strict and demanding standard applied by the Supreme Court in *Sutton* and *Toyota*."[21] However, the Senate rejected the use of the term "materially restricts," concluding that "adopting a new, undefined term that is subject to widely disparate meanings is not the best way to achieve the goal of ensuring consistent and appropriately broad coverage under this Act."[22] In passing the Senate bill, House debate indicated that although the term "materially restricts" was not ultimately adopted, the intent was the same as that of the Senate language. Thus, House debate stated that the descriptions of the changes intended by the term "materially restricts" in the House Committee Reports should be read as what is intended by the language of P.L. 110-325.[23]

The ADA Amendments Act specifically lists examples of major life activities including caring for oneself, performing manual tasks, seeing, hearing, eating, sleeping, walking, standing, lifting, bending, speaking, breathing, learning, reading, concentrating, thinking, communicating, and working. The act also states that a major life activity includes the operation of a major bodily function. The House Judiciary Committee report indicates that "this clarification was needed to ensure that the impact of an impairment on the operation of major bodily functions is not overlooked or wrongly dismissed as falling outside the definition of 'major life activities' under the ADA."[24] There had been judicial decisions which found that certain bodily functions had not been covered by the definition of disability. For example, in *Furnish v. SVI Sys., Inc.*[25] the Seventh Circuit held that an individual with cirrhosis of the liver due to infection with Hepatitis B was not an individual with a disability because liver function was not "integral to one's daily existence."

The House debate contains a colloquy between Representatives Pete Stark and George Miller on the subject of the meaning of "substantially limits" in the context of learning, reading, writing, thinking, or speaking. The colloquy finds that an individual who has performed well academically may still be considered an individual with a disability. Representative Stark stated the following:

> Specific learning disabilities, such as dyslexia, are neurologically based impairments that substantially limit the way these individuals perform major life activities, like reading or learning, or the time it takes to perform such activities often referred to as

the condition, manner, or duration. This legislation will reestablish coverage for these individuals by ensuring that the definition of this ability is broadly construed and the determination does not consider the use of mitigating measures.[26]

The EEOC's proposed regulations echo this colloquy, specifically stating that

An individual with a learning disability who is substantially limited in reading, learning, thinking, or concentrating compared to most people, as indicated by the speed or ease with which he can read, the time and effort required for him to learn, or the difficulty he experiences in concentrating or thinking, is an individual with a disability, even if he has achieved a high level of academic success, such as graduating from college. The determination of whether an individual has a disability does not depend on what an individual is able to do in spite of an impairment.[27]

What it means to be substantially limited in working was also addressed by the EEOC proposed regulations. The EEOC noted that usually an individual with a disability will be substantially limited in another major life activity so that it would be unnecessary to determine whether the individual was substantially limited regarding working. However, where that is not the case, the EEOC proposed that "[a]n impairment substantially limits the major life activity of working if it substantially limits an individual's ability to perform, or to meet the qualifications for, the type of work at issue."[28] The EEOC also stated that this interpretation is to be construed broadly and should "not demand extensive analysis."[29]

Regarded as Having a Disability

The third prong of the definition of disability covers individuals who are "regarded as having such an impairment (as described in paragraph (3))." Paragraph 3 states that "[a]n individual meets the requirement of 'being regarded as having such an impairment' if the individual establishes that he or she has been subjected to an action prohibited under this Act because of an actual or perceived physical or mental impairment whether or not the impairment limits or is perceived to limit a major life activity." However, impairments that are transitory and minor are specifically excluded from the regarded prong. A transitory impairment is one with an actual or expected duration of six months or less. The ADA Amendments Act also provides in a rule of construction in Title V of the ADA that a covered entity under Title I,[30] a public entity under Title II, or a person who operates a place of public accommodation under Title III, need not provide a reasonable accommodation or a reasonable modification to policies, practices, or procedures to an individual who meets the definition of disability solely under the "regarded as" prong of the definition.[31]

The Senate Statement of Managers notes that there were some reservations about this change but that it was included "given our strong expectation that ... individuals [who had been given reasonable accommodations under the 'regarded as' prong by courts] would now be covered under the first prong of the definition, properly applied."[32] The House debate echoed the Senate interpretation and expanded on congressional intent, stating the following:

We, and the Senate, expressed our confidence that individuals who need accommodations will receive them because, with reduction in the burden of showing a "substantial limitation," those individuals also qualify for coverage under prongs 1 or 2 (where accommodation still is required). Of course, our clarification here does not shield qualification standards, tests, or other selection criteria from challenge by an individual who is disqualified based on such standard, test, or criteria. As is currently required under the ADA, any standard, test, or other selection criteria that results in disqualification of an individual because of an impairment can be challenged by that individual and must be shown to be job-related and consistent with business necessity for necessary for the program or service in question.[33]

Employment-Related Provisions

The ADA Amendments Act amended Section 102 of the ADA to "mirror the structure of [the] nondiscrimination protection provision in Title VII of the Civil Rights Act of 1964."[34] The act strikes the prohibition of discrimination against a qualified individual with a disability because of the disability of such individual and substitutes the prohibition of discrimination against a qualified individual "on the basis of disability." The Senate Managers' Statement noted that this change "ensures that the emphasis in questions of disability discrimination is properly on the critical inquiry of whether a qualified person has been discriminated against on the basis of disability, and not unduly focused on the preliminary question of whether a particular person is a 'person with a disability.'"[35]

P.L. 110-325 also provides that covered entities may not use qualification standards based on an individual's uncorrected vision unless the standard is shown to be job related and consistent with business necessity.

Rules of Construction

The ADA Amendments Act makes several additions to Title V of the ADA. The act states that the ADA does not alter eligibility standards for benefits under state workers' compensation laws or under state or federal disability benefit programs. P.L. 110-325 also states that nothing in the act alters the provision of Section 302(b)(2)(A)(ii),[36] specifying that reasonable modifications in policies, practices, or procedures shall be required, unless an entity can demonstrate that making such modifications in policies, practices, or procedures, including academic requirements in postsecondary education, would fundamentally alter the nature of the goods, services, facilities, privileges, advantages, or accommodations involved. The Senate Statement of Managers notes that this provision was added at the request of the higher education community and "is included solely to provide assurances that the bill does not alter current law with regard to the obligations of academic institutions under the ADA, which we believe is already demonstrated in case law on this topic."[37] The Managers' Statement also noted that this provision "is unrelated to the purpose of this legislation and should be given no meaning in interpreting the definition of disability."[38]

The ADA Amendments Act specifically prohibits reverse discrimination claims and states that nothing in the act shall provide the basis for a claim by a person without a disability that he or she was subject to discrimination because of a lack of a disability. The Senate Statement of Managers observes that the intent of this provision is "to clarify that a person without a disability does not have the right under the Act to bring an action against an entity on the grounds that he or she was discriminated against 'on the basis of disability.'"[39]

As was discussed previously, the rules of construction provide that a covered entity under Title I, a public entity under Title II, or a person who operates a place of public accommodation under Title III, need not provide a reasonable accommodation or a reasonable modification to policies, practices, or procedures to an individual who meets the definition of disability solely under the "regarded as" prong of the definition.

Regulatory Authority

The Supreme Court in *Sutton* questioned the authority of regulatory agencies to promulgate regulations for the definition of disability in the ADA. The definition of disability is contained in Section 3 of the ADA, and the ADA does not specifically give any agency the authority to interpret the definitions in Section 3, including the definition of disability. The Supreme Court declined to address this issue since, as both parties to *Sutton* accepted the regulation as valid, "we have no occasion to consider what deference they are due, if any." The ADA Amendments Act specifically grants regulatory authority and states that "[t]he authority to issue regulations granted to the Equal Employment Opportunity Commission, the Attorney General, and the Secretary of Transportation under this Act, includes the authority to issue regulations implementing the definitions contained in sections 3 and 4."

Conforming Amendment

The Rehabilitation Act is amended by the ADA Amendments Act to reference the definition of disability in the ADA. The Senate Statement of Managers noted the importance of maintaining uniform definitions in the two statutes so covered entities "will generally operate under one consistent standard, and the civil rights of individuals with disabilities will be protected in all settings."[40] The Senate Statement of Managers also stated the following:

> We expect that the Secretary of Education will promulgate new regulations related to the definition of disability to be consistent with those issued by the Attorney General under this Act. We believe that other current regulations issued by the Department of Education Office of Civil Rights under Section 504 of the Rehabilitation Act are currently harmonious with Congressional intent under both the ADA and the Rehabilitation Act.[41]

Effective Date

The effective date of the ADA Amendments Act is January 1, 2009.

JUDICIAL DECISIONS UNDER THE ADA AMENDMENTS ACT

Since the ADA Amendments Act became effective January 1, 2009, there have been a number of judicial decisions which have sought to allege violations of the ADA as it is amended by the ADAAA. These cases usually have involved fact patterns that took place prior to the ADAAA's effective date, and courts have followed the general rule that, absent clear congressional intent, a statute enacted after the events at issue in a suit does not apply.[42] However, in *Jenkins v. National Board of Medical Examiners,*[43] the plaintiff sought accommodations on the U.S. Medical Licensing Examination and the Sixth Circuit found that the ADAAA did apply. The court reasoned that since the plaintiff was seeking prospective relief (i.e., accommodations for an examination in the future), there was no injustice to the defendant. The case was remanded for consideration and provides no guidance on the substantive interpretation of the ADAAA.[44]

Although the vast majority of ADA Amendments Act cases still turn on the issue of retroactivity, there are a few district court cases addressing the merits of an ADA Amendments Act issue. In *Hoffman v. Carefirst of Fort Wayne, Inc.,*[45] the district court stated that it had "tried in vain" to find relevant case law, noting that this was one of the first cases of its kind. The central issue in *Hoffman* was whether an individual whose cancer is in remission is an individual with a disability under the ADA as amended. Finding that the plaintiff was an individual with a disability, the court observed that the ADA's amended language specifically provides that an impairment that is in remission is a disability if it would substantially limit a major life activity when active and that the question of whether an individual has a disability "should not demand extensive analysis." Interestingly, the court found this conclusion further bolstered by the EEOC's proposed regulations which provide that cancer is an example of an impairment that will consistently meet the definition of disability and that cancer is an example of an impairment that can be in remission.

There will undoubtedly be more cases involving the ADA Amendments Act. The EEOC announced on September 9, 2010, that it was filing suit in three cases using the new definition of disability.[46] These cases involved individuals with diabetes, cancer, and severe arthritis.

End Notes

[1] 42 U.S.C. §§12101 et seq. For a more detailed discussion of the ADA, see CRS Report 98-921, *The Americans with Disabilities Act (ADA): Statutory Language and Recent Issues,* by Nancy Lee Jones.

[2] 42 U.S.C. §12101(b)(1).

[3] *Sutton v. United Air Lines, Inc.,* 527 U.S. 471 (1999); *Murphy v. United Parcel Service, Inc.,* 527 U.S. 516 (1999); *Kirkingburg v. Albertson's Inc.,* 527 U.S. 555 (1999); *Toyota Motor Manufacturing v. Williams,* 534 U.S. 184 (2002).

[4] 74 FED. REG.. 48431 (September 23, 2009).

[5] Section 504, 29 U.S.C. §794, prohibits discrimination based on disability in any program or activity receiving federal funds or in the executive branch or the U.S. Postal Service. The applicable definition of disability is codified at 29 U.S.C. §706(8).

[6] P.L. 101-336, §3(2).

[7] 297 F.3d 720 (8th Cir. 2002), cert. denied, 571 U.S. 1070 (2004).

[8] 75 Fed. Appx. 983 (5th Cir. 2003).

[9] 231 Fed. Appx. 874 (11th Cir. 2007), cert. denied, 128 S.Ct. 302, 169 L.Ed.2d 247 (October 1, 2007). For a discussion of other lower court cases see National Council on Disability, "The Impact of the Supreme Court's ADA Decisions on the Rights of Persons With Disabilities," February 25, 2003, http://www.ncd.gov/newsroom/publications/2003/ decisionsimpact.htm.

[10] 231 Fed. Appx. 874, 877 (11th Cir. 2007), cert. denied, 128 S.Ct. 302, 169 L.Ed.2d 247 (October 1, 2007).

[11] In the 109th Congress, Representatives Sensenbrenner, Hoyer, and Conyers introduced H.R. 6258, 109th Cong., 2d Sess., to amend the definition of disability.

[12] "Restoring Congressional Intent and Protections under the Americans with Disabilities Act," Before the Senate Committee on Health, Education, Labor, and Pensions, November 15, 2007, http://help.senate.gov/Hearings/2007_11_15_b/2007_11_15_b.html.

[13] Hearing on H.R. 3195, the ADA Restoration Act of 2007, Before the House Committee on the Judiciary, Subcommittee on the Constitution, Civil Rights, and Civil Liberties, October 4, 2007, http://judiciary.house.gov/ Hearings.aspx?ID=182.

[14] "H.R. 3195: The ADA Restoration Act of 2007," Before the House Committee on Education and Labor, January 29, 2008, http://edlabor.house.gov/hearings/fc-2008-01-29.shtml.

[15] The changes were a result of extensive negotiations between the business community and national disability organizations. See discussions of this process at 153 Cong. Rec. S. 8350 (Sept. 11, 2008)(Statement of Senator Harkin); 153 CONG. REC. H. 8294 (September 17, 2008)(Statement of Representatives Hoyer and Sensenbrenner).

[16] "Determining the Proper Scope of Coverage for the Americans with Disabilities Act," Before the Senate Committee on Health, Education, Labor, and Pensions, July 15, 2008, http://help.senate.gov/Hearings/2008_07_15/ 2008_07_15.html.

[17] 153 Cong. Rec. S. 8356 (Sept. 11, 2008). For the Statement of Managers to Accompany S. 3406 see 153 Cong. Rec. S. 8344 (Sept. 11, 2008).

[18] P.L. 110-325, §4(a), amending 42 U.S.C. §12102(3). The ADA Amendments Act does not specifically list covered disabilities, but the EEOC proposed regulations do provide examples of impairments that will consistently meet the definition of disability, including autism, cancer, cerebral palsy, diabetes, epilepsy, HIV or AIDS, multiple sclerosis and muscular dystrophy, major depression, bipolar disorder, post-traumatic stress disorder, obsessive compulsive disorder, and schizophrenia. EEOC Proposed Regulations, to be codified at 29 C.F.R. § 1630.2(j)(5); 74 FED. REG. 48441 (September 23, 2009). The EEOC proposed regulations also noted some impairments that are usually not considered to be disabilities, stating the following: "[t]emporary, non-chronic impairments of short duration with little or no residual effects (such as the common cold, seasonal or common influenza, a sprained joint, minor and non-chronic gastrointestinal disorders, or a broken bone that is expected to heal completely) usually will not substantially limit a major life activity." EEOC Proposed Regulations, to be codified at 29 C.F.R. § 1630.2(j)(8); 74 FED. REG.. 48443 (September 23, 2009).

[19] Low vision devices are not included in the ordinary eyeglasses and contact lens exception.

[20] EEOC Proposed Regulations, to be codified at 29 C.F.R. § 1630.2(j)(1); 74 FED. REG.. 48440 (September 23, 2009).

[21] 153 Cong. Rec. S. 8345 (Sept. 11, 2008)(Statement of Managers to Accompany S. 3406, the Americans with Disabilities Act Amendments Act of 2008).

[22] Id.

[23] 153 Cong. Rec. H.8294 (September 17, 2008).

[24] H.Rept. 110-730, Part 2, at 16 (2008).

[25] 270 F.3d 445 (7th Cir. 2001).

[26] 153 Cong. Rec. H. 8291 (September 17, 2008).

[27] EEOC Proposed Regulations, to be codified at 29 C.F.R. § 1630.2(j)(6)(C); 74 FED. REG. . 48442 (September 23, 2009).

[28] EEOC Proposed Regulations, to be codified at 29 C.F.R. § 1630.2(j)(7); 74 FED. REG. . 48442 (September 23, 2009).

[29] Id.

[30] Title I of the ADA covers employment, title II covers states and localities, and title III covers places of public accommodations such as grocery stores, doctors' offices, and movie theaters.

[31] Under previous law, the circuits were split on whether there is a duty to accommodate a "regarded as" plaintiff. See e.g., D'Angelo v.ConAgra Foods, Inc., 422 F.3d 1220 (11th Cir. 2005)(duty to accommodate); Kaplan v. City of North Las Vegas, 323 F.3d 1226 (9th Cir. 2003), cert. denied, 540 U.S. 1049 (2003)(no duty to accommodate).

[32] 153 Cong. Rec. S. 8347 (Sept. 11, 2008)(Statement of Managers to Accompany S. 3406, the Americans with Disabilities Act Amendments Act of 2008).

[33] 153 Cong. Rec. H. 8290 (September 17, 2008).

[34] 153 Cong. Rec. S. 8347 (Sept. 11, 2008)(Statement of Managers to Accompany S. 3406, the Americans with Disabilities Act Amendments Act of 2008).

[35] Id.

[36] 42 U.S.C. §12182(b)(2)(A)(ii).

[37] 153 Cong. Rec. S. 8347 (Sept. 11, 2008)(Statement of Managers to Accompany S. 3406, the Americans with Disabilities Act Amendments Act of 2008).

[38] Id.

[39] *Id.*

[40] *Id.*

[41] *Id.*

[42] See e.g., *EEOC v. Agro Distribution, LLC,* 555 F.3d 462 (5th Cir. 2009).

[43] 2009 U.S. App. LEXIS 2660 (6th Cir. Feb. 11, 2009).

[44] For a discussion of the possible impact of the ADA Amendments Act on schools see Wendy F. Hensel, "Rights Resurgence: The Impact of the ADA Amendments Act on Schools and Universities," 25 Ga. St. U. L. Rev. 641 (2009).

[45] 2010 U.S. Dist. LEXIS 90879 (N.D. Ind. Aug. 31, 2010). See also *Broderick v. Research Foundation of State University of New York,* 2010 U.S. Dist. LEXIS 82031 (Aug. 11, 2010), where the court, noting the new, broader definition of disability, found that the plaintiff failed to state a claim since she did not explain what major life activity was effected by her hip and lower back injury.

[46] http://www.eeoc.gov/eeoc/newsroom/release/9-9-10a.cfm.

In: The Americans with Disabilities Act (ADA): Provisions...   ISBN: 978-1-61470-961-9
Editor: John Kiviniemi and Cécile Sanjo   © 2012 Nova Science Publishers, Inc.

Chapter 3

THE AMERICANS WITH DISABILITIES ACT (ADA): FINAL RULE AMENDING TITLE II AND TITLE III REGULATIONS

Nancy Lee Jones

SUMMARY

The Americans with Disabilities Act (ADA) has as its purpose "to provide a clear and comprehensive national mandate for the elimination of discrimination against individuals with disabilities." On July 26, 2010, the 20th anniversary of the passage of the ADA, the Department of Justice (DOJ) issued final rules amending the existing regulations under ADA title II (prohibiting discrimination against individuals with disabilities by state and local governments) and ADA title III (prohibiting discrimination against individuals with disabilities by places of public accommodations). The new regulations for title II and title III are similar. They both adopt accessibility standards consistent with the minimum guidelines and requirements issued by the Architectural and Transportation Barriers Compliance Board (Access Board). In addition, the regulations include more detailed standards for service animals and power-driven mobility devices, ticketing, effective communication, and provide for an element-by-element "safe harbor" in certain circumstances. The regulations take effect March 15, 2011, but compliance with the 2010 standards for accessible design is not required until March 15, 2012. These final regulations only address issues that were in the 2008 notice of proposed rulemaking. DOJ has noted that it intends to engage in additional rulemaking in certain areas, including equipment and furniture, next generation 9-1-1, movie captioning and video description, and accessibility of websites operated by public entities or places of public accommodation.

INTRODUCTION

The Americans with Disabilities Act (ADA) has often been described as the most sweeping nondiscrimination legislation since the Civil Rights Act of 1964. As stated in the act, its purpose is "to provide a clear and comprehensive national mandate for the elimination of discrimination against individuals with disabilities."[1] On July 26, 2010, the 20th anniversary of the passage of the ADA, the Department of Justice (DOJ) issued final rules amending the existing regulations under ADA title II (prohibiting discrimination against individuals with disabilities by state and local governments) and ADA title III (prohibiting discrimination against individuals with disabilities by places of public accommodations).[2] The new regulations for title II and title III are similar. They both adopt accessibility standards consistent with the minimum guidelines and requirements issued by the Architectural and Transportation Barriers Compliance Board (Access Board). In addition, the regulations include more detailed standards for service animals and power-driven mobility devices, ticketing, and effective communication, and provide for an element-by-element "safe harbor" in certain circumstances. The regulations take effect March 15, 2011, but compliance with the 2010 standards for accessible design is not required until March 15, 2012. These final regulations only address issues that were in the 2008 notice of proposed rulemaking. DOJ has noted that it intends to engage in additional rulemaking in certain areas, including equipment and furniture, movie captioning and video description, next generation 9-1-1, and accessibility of websites operated by public entities or places of public accommodation.[3]

BACKGROUND

DOJ originally issued title II and title III regulations for the ADA on July 26, 1991. Appendix A to these regulations contained the ADA standards for accessible design that were based on the guidelines published by the Access Board. After a long process that included extensive involvement by DOJ, the Access Board published new guidelines in 2004. DOJ published an advance notice of proposed rulemaking in 2004,[4] and a notice of proposed rulemaking in 2008.[5] Final regulations, adopting the Access Board guidelines and making other changes to the original regulations, were issued on July 26, 2010, and published in the Federal Register on September 15, 2010.[6] Once the DOJ regulations become effective, the 2004 Access Board guidelines "will have legal effect with respect to the Department's title II and title III regulations and will cease to be mere guidance for those areas regulated by the Department."[7]

MAJOR CHANGES TO BOTH THE TITLE II AND TITLE III REGULATIONS

Adoption of Access Board Accessibility Guidelines

The DOJ regulations for titles II and III adopt, with some specific modifications, the Access Board's ADA accessibility guidelines.[8] Changes from previous guidelines are made regarding public facilities and recreational facilities. With regard to public facilities, there are specific requirements for detention and correctional facilities, judicial facilities, and residential dwelling units. Detention and correctional facilities must make accessible at least one of each type of general holding cells, general housing cells, medical care facilities, and visiting areas, while judicial facilities are required to make each courtroom accessible. Residential dwelling units are required to conform to certain accessibility requirements.

Recreational facilities have detailed requirements for amusement rides, recreational boating facilities, exercise machines and equipment, fishing piers and platforms, golf facilities (including miniature golf), play areas, swimming pools, wading pools, and spas, saunas, and steam rooms. For example, at least 50% of all holes on a miniature golf course must be accessible, and these accessible holes must be consecutive.

Safe Harbor

The adoption of the Access Board guidelines increases accessibility; however, DOJ expressed concern about the potential effect of these changes on existing structures. To address these concerns, DOJ added controversial "element-by-element safe harbor" provisions for both titles II and III.

For title II, which applies to states and localities, individuals with disabilities must be provided access to programs "when viewed in their entirety."[9] Unlike title III, then, a public entity under title II is not required to make each of its existing facilities accessible. However, in order to provide "an important measure of clarity and certainty for public entities,"[10] DOJ's title II regulations add a "safe harbor" provision where elements in covered facilities that were built or altered in accordance with the previous 1991 accessibility standards would not be required to be brought into compliance with the new standards until the elements were subject to a planned alteration. DOJ described the safe harbor rule as "a narrow one" but many advocacy groups objected to the proposal, seeing "no basis for 'grandfathering' outdated accessibility standards given the flexibility inherent in the program access standard."[11] On the other hand, public entities supported the safe harbor provision, noting that "it would be an ineffective use of public funds to update buildings to retrofit elements that had already been constructed or modified to department-issued and sanctioned specifications."[12] In addition, safe harbor provisions were adopted regarding the "path of travel" to an altered area. With regard to the path of travel safe harbor, DOJ noted that it is not a blanket exception, and that the provision strikes a balance between the rights of individuals with disabilities and the financial burdens on public entities.[13]

Title III of the ADA, which covers places of public accommodation, requires each covered facility to be accessible but only to the extent that accessibility changes are "readily achievable."[14] The new regulations for title III, like those for title II, also contain a "safe harbor" provision. However, the title III safe harbor provisions differ from what had been proposed. The notice of proposed rulemaking had included a level of barrier removal expenses at which small businesses would be considered to have met their readily achievable barrier removal obligations. This proposal was not included in the final rule since the business community objected to the use of a safe harbor based on net revenue, and the disability community generally opposed its use as contrary to the intent and language of the ADA.[15] However, an element-by-element safe harbor provision, like that in the title II provisions, was included. The new title III regulations provide that elements in covered facilities that were built or altered in compliance with the 1991 standards would not be required to be modified in order to comply with the new standards until the elements were subject to a planned alteration. A similar safe harbor applies to elements associated with the path of travel to an altered area. Generally, DOJ describes the aim of title III's architectural barriers provisions as requiring businesses to make their facilities fully accessible during new construction or renovation and to impose a lesser requirement on businesses that are not changing their facilities.[16] DOJ stated that these goals were met by the inclusion in the rule of a general safe harbor provision.[17]

Service Animals

In its discussion of the proposed regulations in 2008, DOJ noted that it received a large number of complaints about service animals and that there was a trend toward the use of wild or exotic animals.[18] Generally, the ADA requires reasonable modifications on policies, practices, or procedures when necessary to avoid discrimination on the basis of disability.[19] The new regulations specifically provide that public entities (title II) and places of public accommodation (title III) shall modify policies, practices, or procedures to permit the use of a service animal by a person with a disability.[20] However, there are exceptions allowing a service animal to be excluded, including where the animal is out of control or not housebroken.

Both the title II and title III regulations define service animal as "any dog that is individually trained to do work or perform tasks for the benefit of an individual with a disability, including a physical, sensory, psychiatric, intellectual, or other mental disability. Other species of animals, whether wild or domestic, trained or untrained, are not service animals for the purposes of this definition."[21] However, public entities (title II) and public accommodations (title III) are required to make reasonable modifications to policies, practices, or procedures to permit the use of a miniature horse if the horse has been individually trained to do work or perform tasks. Previously, service animal had been defined under title III as "any guide dog, signal dog, or other animal individually trained to do work or perform tasks for the benefit of an individual with a disability."[22] A public entity or place of public accommodation may not ask about the nature or extent of an individual's disability but may ask two questions to determine if the animal is a service animal when it is not readily apparent. These questions are, if the animal is required because of a disability, and what work or task the animal is trained to do.[23]

The new regulations note that the tasks performed by the animal must be directly related to the disability, and the regulations provide examples of the types of work or tasks included. These examples include assisting individuals who are blind or have low vision, assisting an individual during a seizure, and helping persons with psychiatric and neurological disabilities by preventing or interrupting impulsive or destructive behaviors. Emotional support or crime deterrence are not considered work or tasks. The exclusion of animals used for emotional support was controversial, especially regarding the use of emotional support animals by current or former members of the military.[24] However, DOJ noted that such animals may be allowed in residential settings or in transportation, stating, "there are situations not governed by the title II and title III regulations, particularly in the context of residential settings and transportation, where there may be a legal obligation to permit the use of animals that do not qualify as service animals under the ADA, but whose presence nonetheless provides necessary emotional support to persons with disabilities."[25]

Wheelchairs and Other Power-Driven Mobility Devices

Since 1990 when the ADA was enacted, the choices of mobility aids for individuals with disabilities have increased dramatically. Individuals with disabilities have used not only the traditional wheelchair but also large wheelchairs with rubber tracks, riding lawn mowers, golf carts, gasoline-powered two-wheeled scooters, all-terrain vehicles, and Segways. DOJ indicated in the notice of proposed rulemaking that it had received inquiries concerning whether these devices need to be accommodated, the impact of these devices on facilities, and personal safety issues.

The final regulations under both titles II and III include sections on mobility devices and take a two-tiered approach. Wheelchairs must be permitted in all areas open to pedestrian use, while power-driven mobility devices are generally permitted subject to certain limitations. The regulations require a public entity under title II or a public accommodation under title III to permit individuals with mobility impairments to use wheelchairs, scooters, walkers, crutches, canes, braces, or other similar devices designed for use by individuals with mobility impairments in areas open to pedestrian use.[26] A public entity under title II or a public accommodation under title III must make reasonable modifications in its policies and procedures to permit the use of other power-driven mobility devices by individuals with disabilities unless it can be demonstrated that the class of other power-driven mobility devices cannot be operated in accordance with legitimate safety requirements, or would create a direct threat, or fundamentally alter the entity's programs.[27] Determining whether a power-driven mobility device is allowed depends on various factors including the following:

- the type, size, weight, dimensions, and speed of the device;
- the facility's volume of pedestrian traffic;
- the facility's design and operational characteristics;
- whether legitimate safety requirements can be established to permit the safe operation of the mobility device; and
- whether the use of the device creates a substantial risk of serious harm to the immediate environment or natural or cultural resources.[28]

A public entity under title II or public accommodation under title III may ask a person using a power-driven mobility device if the mobility device is required because of the person's disability, but may not ask questions about the person's disability.

Ticketing

The new regulations contain detailed requirements in both titles II and III regarding the sale of tickets for accessible seating. Although the ADA's general prohibitions against discrimination would cover ticketing procedures, DOJ noted violations of the ADA and determined that explicit guidance was necessary.[29] Generally, the regulations require modifications in policies, practices or procedures to ensure that individuals with disabilities can purchase tickets for accessible seating in the same manner as individuals without disabilities.[30] DOJ also includes a provision intended to prevent the fraudulent purchase of tickets for accessible seating, although proof of a disability may not be required.[31]

Effective Communication

Public entities (title II) and public accommodations (title III) are required to ensure that communications with individuals with disabilities are as effective as communication with individuals who do not have disabilities.[32] This requirement includes an obligation to provide effective communication to companions who are individuals with disabilities.[33] The new regulations also specifically provide that video remote interpreting (VRI) may be used to provide effective communication and provide performance standards to ensure that VRI is effective.[34] VRI is a fee based service that uses videoconferencing to allow an individual who is hearing impaired to view and sign to a live interpreter who is in another location. These regulatory provisions are particularly significant in the hospital setting.[35]

MAJOR CHANGES SPECIFIC TO THE TITLE II REGULATIONS

The new regulations for title II contain several provisions specific to title II. These include accessibility requirements for certain residential dwelling units,[36] as well as accessibility requirements for correctional facilities.[37]

MAJOR CHANGES SPECIFIC TO THE TITLE III REGULATIONS

Public accommodations under title III have several new requirements concerning places of lodging. There are specific procedures regarding reservations for places of lodging to ensure that individuals with disabilities can make reservations for accessible guest rooms during the same hours and in the same manner as individuals who do not need accessible rooms.[38] In addition, the definition of "place of public accommodation" is amended to include facilities that operate like hotels.[39] These may include timeshares and condominium properties.[40] In addition, when considering requests for accommodations in examinations or courses, "considerable weight" must be given to the documentation of past modifications in similar situations or the services provided in response to an individualized education plan (IEP) under the Individuals with Disabilities Education Act (IDEA), 20 U.S.C. §1400 et seq.[41]

End Notes

[1] 42 U.S.C. §12101(b)(1).

[2] The regulations were published in the Federal Register on September 15, 2010. 75 FED. REG. 56164 (September 15, 2010).

[3] *Id.* An advance notice of proposed rulemaking seeking comments on these issues has been published. See http://www.ada.gov/anprm2010.htm. For a discussion of the ADA and the internet see CRS Report R40462, *The Americans with Disabilities Act: Application to the Internet*, by Nancy Lee Jones.

[4] 69 FED. REG. 58768 (September 30, 2004).

[5] 73 FED. REG. 34508 (June 17, 2008).

[6] 75 FED. REG. 56164 (September 15, 2010).

[7] *Id.* at 56165.

[8] For a more detailed overview of the major changes see http://www.ada.gov/regs2010/factsheets/2010_Standards_factsheet.html.

[9] 28 C.F.R. §35.150(a).

[10] 75 FED. REG. 56207 (September 15, 2010).

[11] *Id.* at 56206-56207.

[12] *Id.* at 56207.

[13] *Id.* at 56212.

[14] 42 U.S.C. §12182(b)(2)(A)(iv).

[15] 75 FED. REG. 56288 - 56289 (September 15, 2010).

[16] *Id* at 56289.

[17] *Id.*

[18] 73 FED. REG. 34473, 34516 (June 17, 2008).

[19] 42 U.S.C. §12131(2) (title II); 42 U.S.C. §12182(b)(2)(A)(ii) (title III).

[20] New 28 C.F.R. §35.136(a) (title II); New 28 C.F.R. §36. 302 (title III). For a more detailed discussion of the requirements regarding service animals see CRS Report R41468, *The Americans with Disabilities Act (ADA) and Service Animals*, by Nancy Lee Jones.

[21] New 28 C.F.R. §35.104 (title II)(emphasis added); New 28 C.F.R. §36.104 (title III)(emphasis added).

[22] 28 C.F.R. §36.104 (2009)(emphasis added).

[23] 35 C.F.R. §35.136(f) 75 FED. REG. . 56178 (September 15, 2010) (title II); 36 C.F.R. §36.302(c)(6), 75 FED. REG. 56251 (September 15, 2010) (title III).

[24] 75 FED. REG. 56194-56195 (September 15, 2010) (title II); 75 FED. REG. . 56269 (September 15, 2010) (title III).

[25] 75 FED. REG. 56195 (September 15, 2010) (title II); 75 FED. REG. . 56269 (September 15, 2010) (title III).

[26] New 28 C.F.R. §35.137 (title II); New 28 C.F.R. §36.311 (title III).

[27] *Id.*

[28] *Id.*

[29] 75 FED. REG. 56201 (September 15, 2010) (title II); 75 FED. REG. 56275 (September 15, 2010) (title III).

[30] New 28 C.F.R. §35.138 (title II); New 28 C.F.R. §36.302(f) (title III).

[31] New 28 C.F.R. §35.138(h)(title II); New 28 C.F.R. §36.302(f)(8) (title III).

[32] New 28 C.F.R. §35.160(a)(1)(title II); New 28 C.F.R. §36.303 (title III).

[33] *Id.*

[34] New 28 C.F.R. §35.160(d)(title II); New 28 C.F.R. §36.303(b) (title III).

[35] For a more detailed discussion of these regulations in the hospital context see CRS Report 97-826, *Americans with Disabilities Act (ADA) Requirements Concerning the Provision of Interpreters by Hospitals and Doctors*, by Nancy Lee Jones.

[36] New 28 C.F.R. §35.151(e).

[37] New 28 C.F.R. §35.152.

[38] New 28 C.F.R. §36.302(e).

[39] New 28 C.F.R. §36.104.

[40] 75 FED. REG. 56304 (September 15, 2010).

[41] New 28 C.F.R. §36.309(b). For a more detailed discussion of IDEA, see CRS Report R40690, *The Individuals with Disabilities Education Act (IDEA): Statutory Provisions and Recent Legal Issues*, by Nancy Lee Jones.

In: The Americans with Disabilities Act (ADA): Provisions...   ISBN: 978-1-61470-961-9
Editor: John Kiviniemi and Cécile Sanjo   © 2012 Nova Science Publishers, Inc.

Chapter 4

THE ADA AMENDMENTS ACT DEFINITION OF DISABILITY: FINAL EEOC REGULATIONS

Nancy Lee Jones

SUMMARY

The ADA Amendment Act (ADAAA), P.L. 110-325, was enacted in 2008 to amend the Americans with Disabilities Act (ADA) definition of disability. On March 25, 2011, the Equal Employment Opportunity Commission (EEOC) issued final regulations implementing the ADAAA. The final regulations track the statutory language of the ADA but also provide several clarifying interpretations. Several of the major regulatory interpretations are, including the operation of major bodily functions in the definition of major life activities; adding rules of construction for when an impairment substantially limits a major life activity and providing examples of impairments that will most often be found to substantially limit a major life activity; interpreting the coverage of transitory impairments; interpreting the use of mitigating measures; and interpreting the "regarded as" prong of the definition.

INTRODUCTION

The ADA Amendment Act (ADAAA), P.L. 110-325, [1] was enacted in 2008 to amend the Americans with Disabilities Act (ADA). The Americans with Disabilities Act (ADA)[2] is a broad civil rights act prohibiting discrimination against individuals with disabilities. As stated in the act, its purpose is "to provide a clear and comprehensive national mandate for the elimination of discrimination against individuals with disabilities."[3] The ADAAA reiterated this purpose, and also emphasized that it was "reinstating a broad scope of protection" for individuals with disabilities.[4]

The threshold issue in any ADA case is whether the individual alleging discrimination is an individual with a disability. Several Supreme Court decisions interpreted the definition of disability, generally limiting its application.[5] Congress responded to these decisions by enacting the ADA Amendments Act, P.L. 110-325, which rejects the Supreme Court and lower court interpretations and amends the ADA to provide broader coverage. Two of the major changes made by the ADA Amendments Act are to expand the current interpretation of when an impairment substantially limits a major life activity (rejecting the Supreme Court's interpretation in *Toyota*), and to require that the determination of whether an impairment substantially limits a major life activity must be made without regard to the use of mitigating measures (rejecting the Supreme Court's decisions in *Sutton*, *Murphy*, and *Kirkingburg*). On March 25, 2011, the Equal Employment Opportunity Commission (EEOC) issued final regulations implementing the ADA Amendments Act.[6]

STATUTORY PROVISIONS

The ADA Amendments Act defines the term disability with respect to an individual as "(A) a physical or mental impairment that substantially limits one or more of the major life activities of such individual; (B) a record of such an impairment; or (C) being regarded as having such an impairment (as described in paragraph (3))."[7] Paragraph (3) discusses the "regarded as" prong of the definition and provides that an individual is "regarded as" having a disability regardless of whether the impairment limits or is perceived to limit a major life activity, and that the "regarded as" prong does not apply to impairments that are transitory and minor.[8] Although this is essentially the same statutory language as was in the original ADA, P.L. 110-325 contains new rules of construction regarding the definition of disability, which provide that

- the definition of disability shall be construed in favor of broad coverage to the maximum extent permitted by the terms of the act;
- the term "substantially limits" shall be interpreted consistently with the findings and purposes of the ADA Amendments Act;
- an impairment that substantially limits one major life activity need not limit other major life activities to be considered a disability;
- an impairment that is episodic or in remission is a disability if it would have substantially limited a major life activity when active; and
- the determination of whether an impairment substantially limits a major life activity shall be made without regard to the ameliorative effects of mitigating measures, except that the ameliorative effects of ordinary eyeglasses or contact lenses shall be considered.[9]

The findings of the ADA Amendments Act include statements indicating a determination that the Supreme Court decisions in *Sutton* and *Toyota* as well as lower court cases had narrowed and limited the ADA from what was originally intended by Congress. P.L. 110-325 specifically states that the then-current Equal Employment Opportunity Commission (EEOC) regulations defining the term "substantially limits" as "significantly restricted" are "inconsistent with congressional intent, by expressing too high a standard."[10]

FINAL EEOC REGULATIONS

Overview

The EEOC issued final ADAAA regulations on March 25, 2011, which will become effective on May 24, 2011.[11] Proposed regulations were published in the Federal Register on September 23, 2009,[12] and the EEOC received over 600 comments and held a series of "Town Hall Listening Sessions."[13] In general, the final regulations streamlined the organization of the proposed regulations, and moved many examples from the regulation to the appendix. The EEOC notes that the appendix will be published in the *Code of Federal Regulations* (CFR), and "will continue to represent the Commission's interpretation of the issues discussed in the regulations, and the Commission will be guided by it when resolving charges of employment discrimination under the ADA."[14] The final regulations track the statutory language of the ADA but also provide several clarifying interpretations. Several of the major regulatory interpretations are as follows:

- including the operation of major bodily functions in the definition of major life activities;
- adding rules of construction for when an impairment substantially limits a major life activity, and providing examples of impairments that will most often be found to substantially limit a major life activity;
- interpreting the coverage of transitory impairments;
- interpreting the use of mitigating measures; and
- interpreting the "regarded as" prong of the definition.

Major Life Activities

The first prong of the statutory definition of disability, referred to by EEOC as "actual disability," provides that an individual with "a physical or mental impairment that substantially limits one or more of the major life activities of such individual"[15] is an individual with a disability. The final regulations provide a list of examples of major life activities.[16] In addition to those listed in the statute (caring for oneself, performing manual tasks, seeing, hearing, eating, sleeping, walking, standing, lifting, bending, speaking, breathing, learning, reading, concentrating, thinking, communicating, and working),[17] the EEOC includes sitting, reaching, and interacting with others.[18]

Major life activities also include major bodily functions.[19] In addition to the statutory examples (functions of the immune system, normal cell growth, digestive, bowel, bladder, neurological, brain, respiratory, circulatory, endocrine, and reproductive functions), the EEOC includes special sense organs, genitourinary, cardiovascular, hemic, lymphatic and musculoskeletal.[20] The final regulations also provide that the operation of a major bodily function includes the operation of an individual organ within a body system.[21]

The EEOC emphasizes that the ADAAA requires an individualized assessment but notes that because of the statute's requirement for broad coverage, some impairments will almost always be determined to be a disability. The final regulations list impairments that fall within this category. They include deafness, blindness, an intellectual disability, missing limbs or mobility impairments requiring the use of a wheelchair, autism, cancer, cerebral palsy, diabetes, epilepsy, HIV infection, multiple sclerosis, muscular dystrophy, major depressive disorder, bipolar disorder, post-traumatic stress disorder, obsessive compulsive disorder, and schizophrenia.[22] In addition, the EEOC provides that the focus when considering whether an activity is a major life activity should be on "how a major life is substantially limited, and not on what outcomes an individual can achieve."[23] For example, the EEOC noted that an individual with a learning disability my achieve a high level of academic success but may be substantially limited in the major life activity of learning.[24]

Substantially Limits a Major Life Activity

The final regulations provide rules of construction to assist in determining whether an impairment substantially limits an individual in a major life activity.[25] Generally, the regulations provide that not every impairment is a disability but an impairment does not have to prevent or severely limit a major life activity to be considered substantially limiting. The term substantially limits is to be broadly construed to provide expansive coverage,[26] and requires an individualized determination.[27]

Transitory Impairments

The ADAAA specifically provides that an impairment that is episodic or in remission is a disability if it would substantially limit a major life activity when active.[28] In its appendix to the regulations, the EEOC states that "[t]he fact that the periods during which an episodic impairments is active and substantially limits a major life activity may be brief or occur infrequently is no longer relevant to determining whether an impairment substantially limits a major life activity."[29] For example, the EEOC notes that an individual with post-traumatic stress disorder who has intermittent flashbacks is substantially limited in brain function and thinking.[30]

Mitigating Measures

A mitigating measure, for example, a wheelchair or medication, eliminates or reduces the symptoms or impact of an impairment. The ADAAA provided that when determining when an impairment substantially limits a major life activity, the ameliorative effects of mitigating measures shall not be used.[31] However, ordinary eyeglasses and contact lenses may be considered.[32] The EEOC final regulations track the statutory language, and also provide that the negative side effects of a mitigating measure may be taken into account in determining whether an individual is an individual with a disability.[33] Although the EEOC would not allow a covered entity to require the use of a mitigating measure, if an individual does not use a mitigating measure, this may affect whether an individual is qualified for a job or poses a direct threat.[34]

Regarded As Having an Impairment

The third prong of the statutory definition of disability is "being regarded as having an impairment."[35] The ADAAA further describes being regarded as having an impairment by stating that an individual meets this prong of the definition "if the individual establishes that he or she has been subjected to an action prohibited under this Act because of an actual or perceived physical or mental impairment whether or not the impairment limits or is perceived to limit a major life activity."[36] The statute also provides that the "regarded as" prong does not apply to transitory or minor impairments, and a transitory impairment is defined as an impairment with an actual or expected duration of six months or less.[37]

The EEOC final regulations echo the statutory language, and encourage the use of the "regarded as" prong when reasonable accommodation is not at issue.[38] The EEOC emphasizes that even if an individual is regarded as having a disability, there is no violation of the ADA unless a covered entity takes a prohibited action, such as not hiring a qualified individual because he or she is regarded as having a disability.[39] A covered entity may challenge a claim under the "regarded as" prong by showing that the impairment is both transitory and minor,[40] or by showing that the individual is not qualified or would pose a direct threat. However, it should be noted that the defense that an impairment is transitory and minor is only available under the "regarded as" prong. The rules of construction discussed previously concerning the first or actual prong specifically state that the effects of an impairment lasting fewer than six months can be substantially limiting.[41]

End Notes

[1] For a more detailed discussion of the statute see CRS Report RL34691, *The ADA Amendments Act: P.L. 110-325*, by Nancy Lee Jones.

[2] 42 U.S.C. §§12101 et seq. For a more detailed discussion of the ADA, see CRS Report 98-921, *The Americans with Disabilities Act (ADA): Statutory Language and Recent Issues*, by Nancy Lee Jones.

[3] 42 U.S.C. §12101(b)(1).

[4] 20 U.S.C. §12101 note.

[5] Sutton v. United Air Lines, Inc., 527 U.S. 471 (1999); Murphy v. United Parcel Service, Inc., 527 U.S. 516 (1999); Kirkingburg v. Albertson's Inc., 527 U.S. 555 (1999); Toyota Motor Manufacturing v. Williams, 534 U.S. 184 (2002).

[6] 76 Fed. Reg. 16978 (March 25, 2011).

[7] P.L. 110-325, §4(a), amending 42 U.S.C. §12102(1).

[8] P.L. 110-325, §3(3), 42 U.S.C. §12102(3).

[9] P.L. 110-325, §3(4), 42 U.S.C. §12102(4). Low vision devices are not included in the ordinary eyeglasses and contact lens exception.

[10] P.L. 110-325, §2(a)(8); 42 U.S.C. §12101 note.

[11] 76 Fed. Reg. 16978 (March 25, 2011).

[12] 74 Fed. Reg. 48431 (September 23, 2009).

[13] 76 Fed. Reg. 16979 (March 25, 2011).

[14] *Id.*

[15] 42 U.S.C. §12102(1).

[16] The EEOC specifically states that these examples are not limiting.

[17] 42 U.S.C. §12102(2)(A).

[18] New 29 C.F.R. §1630.2(i)(1)(i); 76 Fed. Reg. 17000 (March 25, 2011).

[19] 42 U.S.C. §12102(2)(B).

[20] New 29 C.F.R. §1630.2(i)(1)(ii); 76 Fed. Reg. 17000 (March 25, 2011).

[21] *Id.*

[22] New 29 C.F.R. §1630.2(j)(3)(iii); 76 Fed. Reg. 17001 (March 25, 2011).

[23] New 29 C.F.R. §1630.2(j)(4)(iii); 76 Fed. Reg. 17001 (March 25, 2011).

[24] *Id.*

[25] New 29 C.F.R. §1630.2(j)(1); 76 FED. REG. 17000 (March 25, 2011).

[26] New 29 C.F.R. §1630.2(j)(1)(i); 76 FED. REG. 17000 (March 25, 2011).

[27] New 29 C.F.R. §1630.2(j)(1)(iv); 76 FED. REG. 17000 (March 25, 2011).

[28] 42 U.S.C. §12102(4)(D).

[29] 76 FED. REG. 17011 (March 25, 2011).

[30] *Id.*

[31] 42 U.S.C. §12102(4)(E).

[32] *Id.*

[33] New 29 C.F.R. §1630.2(j)(4)(ii); 76 FED. REG. 17001 (March 25, 2011).

[34] 76 FED. REG. 17010 (March 25, 2011).

[35] 42 U.S.C. §12102(1)(C).

[36] 42 U.S.C. §12102(3)(A).

[37] 42 U.S.C. §12102(3)(B).

[38] New 29 C.F.R. §1630.2(g)(3); 76 FED. REG. 17000 (March 25, 2011).

[39] New 29 C.F.R. §1630.2(l); 76 FED. REG. 17002 (March 25, 2011).

[40] New 29 C.F.R. §1630.15(f); 76 FED. REG. 17003 (March 25, 2011).

[41] New 29 C.F.R. §1630.2(j)(1)(ix); 76 FED. REG. 17000 (March 25, 2011).

In: The Americans with Disabilities Act (ADA): Provisions…   ISBN: 978-1-61470-961-9
Editor: John Kiviniemi and Cécile Sanjo   © 2012 Nova Science Publishers, Inc.

Chapter 5

THE AMERICANS WITH DISABILITIES ACT: LEGISLATION CONCERNING NOTIFICATION PRIOR TO INITIATING LEGAL ACTION

Nancy Lee Jones

SUMMARY

The Americans with Disabilities Act (ADA) provides broad nondiscrimination protection in employment, public services, and public accommodation and services operated by private entities. Since the 106th Congress, legislation has been introduced to require plaintiffs to provide notice to the defendant prior to filing a complaint regarding public accommodations. In the 112th Congress, H.R. 881 was introduced by Representative Hunter to amend Title III of the ADA to require notification.

INTRODUCTION

The Americans with Disabilities Act[1] has often been described as the most sweeping nondiscrimination legislation since the Civil Rights Act of 1964. It provides broad nondiscrimination protection and, as stated in the act, its purpose is "to provide a clear and comprehensive national mandate for the elimination of discrimination against individuals with disabilities."[2] Title III of the ADA prohibits discrimination against individuals with disabilities by places of public accommodations, and has been the basis of numerous legal actions. Several of these have involved the filing of multiple law suits by an individual with a disability based on de minimus violations. Of the actions which have resulted in judicial decisions, some have rejected the allegations, finding that the plaintiff was a vexatious litigant, while others have rejected the suits finding that the plaintiff had no standing since the plaintiff could not establish an intent to return to the entity with the alleged ADA violations. Some courts, however, have upheld the plaintiff's action even where numerous previous suits had been filed. Legislation has been introduced since the 106th Congress to require that a plaintiff provide notice of non compliance with the ADA to an entity prior to commencing a legal action.

THE AMERICANS WITH DISABILITIES ACT

Statutory Provisions

Title III of the ADA provides that no individual shall be discriminated against on the basis of disability in the full and equal enjoyment of the goods, services, facilities, privileges, advantages, or accommodations of any place of public accommodation by any person who owns, leases (or leases to), or operates a place of public accommodation.[3] Entities covered by the term "public accommodation" are listed and include, among others, hotels, restaurants, theaters, auditoriums, laundromats, museums, parks, zoos, private schools, day care centers, professional offices of health care providers, and gymnasiums.[4] Although the sweep of Title III is broad, there are some limitations on its nondiscrimination requirements. A failure to remove architectural barriers is not a violation unless such a removal is "readily achievable."[5] "Readily achievable" is defined as "easily accomplishable and able to be carried out without much difficulty or expense."[6] Reasonable modifications in practices, policies or procedures are required unless they would fundamentally alter the nature of the goods, services, facilities, or privileges.[7] No individual with a disability may be excluded, denied services, segregated or otherwise treated differently than other individuals because of the absence of auxiliary aids and services unless the entity can demonstrate that taking such steps would fundamentally alter the nature of the goods, services, or facilities or would result in an undue burden.[8] An undue burden is defined as an action involving "significant difficulty or expense."[9]

The remedies and procedures of section 204(a) of the Civil Rights Act of 1964 are incorporated in Title III of the ADA.[10] This allows for both private suit and suit by the Attorney General when there is reasonable cause to believe that there is a pattern or practice of discrimination against individuals with disabilities. Monetary damages are not recoverable in private suits but may be available in suits brought by the Attorney General.[11] Section 204(c) of the Civil Rights Act requires that when there is a state or local law prohibiting an action also prohibited by Title II, no civil action may be brought "before the expiration of thirty days after written notice of such alleged act or practice has been given to the appropriate State or local authority...." The ADA does not specifically incorporate this requirement, and the courts which have considered the issue have generally found that this requirement was not incorporated in the ADA.[12]

Judicial Decisions

Although situations involving the filing of multiple law suits by an individual with a disability based on de minimus violations have generally been settled out of court, there have been judicial decisions involving these issues.[13] Generally, the cases that have gone to court have addressed questions concerning whether the plaintiff is a vexatious litigant or whether the plaintiff has standing.

In *Molski v. Mandarin Touch Restaurant*[14] a California district court found that the plaintiff was a vexatious litigant who filed hundreds of law suits designed to harass and intimidate business owners into agreeing to cash settlements.[15] The plaintiff, Jack Molski, had a physical disability which required that he use a wheelchair and had filed between 300-400 lawsuits in federal courts since 1998. The district court reviewed the cases and found that "many are nearly identical in terms of the facts alleged, the claims presented, and the damages requested."[16] In fact, the court noted in one complaint Mr. Molski claimed that on May 20, 2003, he went to El 7 Mares restaurant which he alleged lacked adequate parking and had a food counter that was too high. After the meal, the plaintiff alleged that he attempted to use the restroom but because the toilet's grab bars were improperly installed, he injured his shoulder and he was also unable to wash his hands due to faulty design. In two other cases, Mr. Molski alleged that he encountered almost identical problems in another restaurant and at a winery on the same day, May 20, 2003. The court found these complaints to be indicative of a clear intent to harass businesses.[17] Even though the court noted that it was "possible, even likely, that many of the businesses sued were not in full compliance with the ADA," the court found the sanctions for bad faith were not therefore barred, especially where the motive was to garner funds. The district court ordered the plaintiff to obtain the leave of the court prior to filing any other claims under the ADA observing that "in addition to misusing a noble law, Molski has plainly lied in his filings to this Court. His claims of being the innocent victim of hundreds of physical and emotional injuries over the last four years defy belief and common sense."[18] In a related suit, the California district court also found against the counsel in the *Molski* case holding that the counsel was required to seek leave of the court before filing any additional ADA claims.[19]

These two cases were upheld on appeal to the ninth circuit in *Molski v. Evergreen Dynasty Corp.*[20] After a detailed examination of the cases in light of standards for vexatious litigation, the ninth circuit noted:

> For the ADA to yield its promise of equal access for the disabled, it may indeed be necessary and desirable for committed individuals to bring serial litigation advancing the time when public accommodations will be compliant with the ADA. But as important as this goal is to disabled individuals and to the public, serial litigation can become vexatious when, as here, a large number of nearly-identical complaints contain factual allegations that are contrived, exaggerated, and defy common sense.[21]

Similarly, the court of appeals held that the district court was within its discretion to impose a pre-filing order. The ninth circuit observed "[t]hat the Frankovich Group filed numerous complaints containing false factual allegations, thereby enabled Molski's vexatious litigation, provided the district court with sufficient grounds on which to base its discretionary imposition of sanctions."[22]

Several courts have addressed the standing issue. Some courts have found that a plaintiff lacks standing to bring an ADA claim for injunctive relief under Title III if the plaintiff cannot establish that he or she intends to return to the entity with the alleged ADA violations. For example, in *Harris v. Stonecrest Care Auto Center,*[23] the district court questioned the plaintiff's credibility due to the fact that he had brought at least twenty other ADA related lawsuits, and carefully examined the requirements of standing. Noting that Title III of the ADA was intended to remedy discrimination in the area of public accommodation by providing injunctive relief, the court concluded that since the plaintiff had visited the gas station "solely for the purpose of bringing a Title III claim and supplemental state claims, any injunctive relief (the court) might grant would not satisfy the redressability requirement of standing."[24] Similarly, in *Tampa Bay Americans with Disabilities Association, Inc. v. Nancy Markoe Gallery, Inc.,*[25] the court found that the plaintiff failed to demonstrate a real and immediate threat of future injury since her visits to the store were infrequent, there was a gap in time between visits, and she did not live in the same city as the store. The court also noted "with some concern" that the Tampa Bay Americans with Disabilities Association had filed 16 previous ADA cases and the individual plaintiff had filed 14.[26] However, in *Hollynn D'Llil v. Best Western Encina Lodge and Suites,*[27] the Ninth Circuit held that the plaintiff's declaration and testimony were sufficient to confer standing despite her past ADA litigation which involved about 60 ADA suits. The court, emphasizing the plaintiff's testimony detailing her intent to return to Santa Barbara and noting her friends who lived there, found that her past litigation did not impugn her credibility.[28]

NOTIFICATION LEGISLATION

Overview

Changes in the ADA's statutory language to address the issue of vexatious law suits have been proposed since the 106th Congress. Proponents of such legislation have argued that notification requirements would help prevent the filing of suits designed to generate money for plaintiffs and law firms.[29] Those opposed to the legislation have argued that it would undermine enforcement of the ADA and that vexatious suits are best dealt with by state bar disciplinary procedures or by the courts.[30]

Legislation in the 111th and 112th Congresses

Representative Hunter introduced H.R. 881, the ADA Notification Act of 2011, 112th Congress, on March 2, 2011. This bill is identical to H.R. 2397 which Representative Hunter introduced in the 111th Congress. H.R. 881 would amend Title III of the ADA to deny state or federal court jurisdiction in a civil action brought under Title III of the ADA, or under a state law that conditions a violation of its provisions on a violation of Title III, except in certain situations. The courts would have jurisdiction if

- a plaintiff provides the defendant written notice of the alleged violation by registered mail prior to filing a complaint;
- the written notice identifies the facts that constitute the alleged violation, including the location and date of the alleged violation;
- a remedial period of 90 days elapses after the date on which the plaintiff provides the written notice;
- the written notice informs the defendant that the plaintiff is barred from filing the complaint until the end of the remedial period; and

- the complaint states that, as of the date on which the complaint is filed, the defendant has not corrected the alleged violation.

H.R. 881 also provides that a court may extend the remedial period by not more than thirty days if the defendant applies for an extension.

Legislation in Previous Congresses

The legislation in previous Congresses is similar, but not identical, to that in the 111th and 112th. H.R. 3479, 110th Congress, and H.R. 2804, 109th Congress, had essentially the same notification provisions as those in H.R. 881, 112th Congress. However, the notification provisions would not have applied to civil actions brought under Rule 65 of the Federal Rules of Civil Procedure or civil actions under state or local court rules requesting preliminary injunctive relief or temporary restraining orders.

H.R. 728, 108th Congress, differed from the more recent legislation by, for example, allowing notice to be provided in person, not just by registered mail. Although the bill was not passed in the 108th Congress, the House Subcommittee on Rural Enterprises, Agriculture, and Technology of the House Small Business Committee held hearings on the bill on April 8, 2003.[31]

The two ADA Notification Acts in the 107th Congress, H.R. 914[32] and S. 792,[33] like their predecessors H.R. 3590[34] and S. 3122,[35] 106th Cong., contained similar language.[36] Hearings were held by the Subcommittee on the Constitution of the House Committee on the Judiciary on H.R. 3590 on May 18, 2000.[37]

End Notes

[1] 42 U.S.C. §§12101 et seq.

[2] 42 U.S.C. §12102(b)(1). For a more detailed discussion of the ADA generally see CRS Report 98-921, *The Americans with Disabilities Act (ADA): Statutory Language and Recent Issues*, by Nancy Lee Jones.

[3] 42 U.S.C. §12182. The Department of Justice amended the regulations promulgated under Title III in 2010. For a discussion of these changes see CRS Report R41376, *The Americans with Disabilities Act (ADA): Final Rule Amending Title II and Title III Regulations*, by Nancy Lee Jones.

[4] 42 U.S.C. §12181.

[5] 42 U.S.C. §12182(b)(2)(A)(iv).

[6] 42 U.S.C. §12181.

[7] 42 U.S.C. §12182(b)(2)(A)(ii).

[8] 42 U.S.C. §12182(b)(2)(A)(iii).

[9] 28 C.F.R. §36.104.

[10] 42 U.S.C. §12188. Section 204a-3(a) of the Civil Rights Act of 1964 is codified at 42 U.S.C. §2000a-3(a).

[11] 42 U.S.C. §12188(b)(4).

[12] See e.g., *Botosan v. Paul McNally Realty*, 216 F.3d 827 (9th Cir. 2000). For a detailed discussion of this issue see Adam A. Milani, "Go Ahead. Make my 90 Days: Should Plaintiffs be Required to Provide Notice to Defendant Before Filing Suit Under Title III of the Americans with Disabilities Act?" 2001 Wisc. L. Rev. 107 (2001). This article argues that the best reading of the ADA is that it requires, like Title II of the Civil Rights Act, that plaintiffs provide thirty days notice to a state or local agency responsible for combating discrimination prior to filing suit. The article concludes that this interpretation renders federal legislation to provide notice unnecessary.

[13] Commentators have also explored these issues. See e.g., Carri Becker, "Private Enforcement of the Americans with Disabilities Act via Serial Litigation: Abusive or Commendable?" 17 HASTINGS WOMEN'S L.J. 93

(2006); Samuel R. Bagenstos, "The Perversity of Limited Civil Rights Remedies: The Case of 'Abusive' ADA Litigation," 54 UCLA L. REV. 1 (2006).

[14] 347 F.Supp.2d 860 (C.D.Calif. 2004).

[15] California has seen several of these cases since, although the ADA only provides for injunctive relief, attorneys' fees, and costs, California state law permit the recovery of money damages. See Cal. Civ. Code §§ 51(f), 54(c), 54.3(a).

[16] *Id.* at 861.

[17] The district court observed: "The Court is tempted to exclaim: 'what a lousy day!' It would be highly unusual—to say the least—for anyone to sustain two injuries, let alone three, in a single day, each of which necessitated a separate federal lawsuit. But in Molski's case, May 20, 2003, was simply business as usual. Molski filed 13 separate complaints for essentially identical injuries sustained between May 19, 2003 and May 23, 2003. The Court simply does not believe that Molski suffered 13 nearly identical injuries, generally to the same part of his body, in the course of performing the same activity, over a five-day period." *Id.* at 865.

[18] 347 F.Supp.2d 860, 867 (C.D.Calif. 2004).

[19] *Molski v. Mandarin Touch Restaurant,* 359 F.Supp 924 (C.D.Calif. 2005). See also *Molski v. Arby's Huntington Beach,* 359 F.Supp.2d 938 (C.D.Calif. 2005).

[20] 500 F.3d 1047 (9th Cir. 2007), cert. denied, 129 S. Ct. 594, 172 L. Ed. 2d 455 (2008).

[21] *Id.* at 38.

[22] *Id.* at 43.

[23] 472 F. Supp.2d 1208 (S.D. Calif. 2007). See also, Fiedler v. Ocean Prop., 683 F.Supp.2d 57 (D.Me. 2010); Access 4 All v. Boardwalk Regency Corp., 2010 U.S. Dist. LEXIS 124625 (D.NJ, Nov. 23, 2010).

[24] *Id.* at 1220.

[25] 2007 U.S.Dist. LEXIS 53866 (M.D. Fla. May 3, 2007).

[26] *Id.* at 6. See also *Steven Brother v. Tiger Partner, LLC,* 331 F.Supp.2d 1368 (M.D. Fla 2004), where the court found a lack of a "continuing connection" to the business being sued but argued for an amendment to the ADA stating that "[o]nly Congress can respond to vexatious litigation tactics that otherwise comply with its statutory frameworks."

[27] 538 F.3d 1031 (9th Cir. 2008).

[28] *Id.* at 1040.

[29] See Testimony of the honorable Mark Foley, hearing on H.R. 3590, The ADA Notification Act, Before the House Committee on the Judiciary, Subcommittee on the Constitution, May 18, 2000. Published at http://www.house.gov/ judiciary/fole0518.htm.

[30] See Letter to Honorable Charles Canady, chairman, Subcommittee on the Constitution, House Committee on the Judiciary from Robert Raben, Assistant Attorney General reprinted at http://commdocs.house.gov/committees/judiciary/hju66728.000/hju66728_0f.htm.

[31] http://wwwc.house.gov/smbiz/hearings/108th/2003/030408/New.asp.

[32] H.R. 914 was introduced by Rep. Foley.

[33] S. 792 was introduced by Sen. Inouye.

[34] H.R. 3590 was introduced by Rep. Foley.

[35] S. 3122 was introduced by Sen. Hutchinson.

[36] H.R. 914, 107th Cong., H.R. 3590, 106th Cong., and S. 3122, 106th Cong. are identical. S. 792 contains some minor differences.

[37] Hearing on H.R. 3590, the ADA Notification Act, Before the House Committee on the Judiciary, Subcommittee on the Constitution, May 18, 2000. http://commdocs.house.gov/committees/judiciary/hju 66728.000/hju66728_0f.htm.

In: The Americans with Disabilities Act (ADA): Provisions...   ISBN: 978-1-61470-961-9
Editor: John Kiviniemi and Cécile Sanjo   © 2012 Nova Science Publishers, Inc.

Chapter 6

THE AMERICANS WITH DISABILITIES ACT AND EMERGENCY PREPAREDNESS AND RESPONSE

Nancy Lee Jones

SUMMARY

The Americans with Disabilities Act (ADA) provides broad nondiscrimination protection for individuals with disabilities in employment, public services, and public accommodations and services operated by private entities. Although the ADA does not include provisions specifically discussing its application to disasters, its nondiscrimination provisions are applicable to emergency preparedness and responses to disasters. In order to further the ADA's goals, President Bush issued an Executive Order on July 22, 2004, relating to emergency preparedness for individuals with disabilities and establishing the Interagency Coordinating Council on Emergency Preparedness and Individuals with Disabilities. The Department of Homeland Security (DHS) issued its Nationwide Plan Review Phase 2 Report, which includes a discussion of people with disabilities and emergency planning and readiness. The National Council on Disability has also issued recommendations on emergency preparation and disaster relief relating to individuals with disabilities. The Post-Katrina Emergency Management Reform Act of 2006 added the position of disability coordinator to FEMA.

INTRODUCTION

According to the U.S. Census Bureau, there are 54.4 million individuals with disabilities in the United States.[1] The challenges faced by these individuals, and their civil rights to inclusion in disaster preparedness and response, have received increased attention after September 11, Hurricane Katrina, and other disasters.[2]

The Americans with Disabilities Act (ADA)[3] provides broad nondiscrimination protection for individuals with disabilities in employment, public services, and public accommodations and services operated by private entities. Although the ADA does not include provisions specifically discussing its application to disasters, its nondiscrimination provisions are applicable to emergency preparedness and responses to disasters. In order to further the ADA's goals, President Bush issued an Executive Order on July 22, 2004, relating to emergency preparedness for individuals with disabilities and establishing the Interagency Coordinating Council on Emergency Preparedness and Individuals with Disabilities. The Department of Homeland Security (DHS) issued its Nationwide Plan Review Phase 2 Report, which includes a discussion of people with disabilities and emergency planning and readiness. The Post-Katrina Emergency Management Reform Act of 2006 added the position of disability coordinator to FEMA. The National Council on Disability has also issued recommendations on emergency preparation and disaster relief relating to individuals with disabilities.

THE AMERICANS WITH DISABILITIES ACT

Statutory and Regulatory Language

The ADA has as its purpose "to provide a clear and comprehensive national mandate for the elimination of discrimination against individuals with disabilities."[4] Although the ADA does not specifically mention disasters, its provisions are broad and would provide nondiscrimination protection.

The definitions in the ADA, particularly the definition of "disability," are the starting point for an analysis of rights provided by the law. The term "disability," with respect to an individual, is defined as "(A) a physical or mental impairment that substantially limits one or more of the major life activities of such individual; (B) a record of such an impairment; or (C) being regarded as having such an impairment (as described in paragraph (3))."[5] The issues involving the definition of disability have been among the most controversial under the ADA. The ADA was amended to expand the interpretation of the definition of disability.[6]

Title I of the ADA provides that no covered entity shall discriminate against a qualified individual on the basis of disability in regard to job application procedures; the hiring, advancement, or discharge of employees; employee compensation; job training; and other terms, conditions, and privileges of employment.[7] Title II of the ADA provides that no qualified individual with a disability shall be excluded from participation in or be denied the benefits of the services, programs, or activities of a public entity or be subjected to discrimination by any such entity.[8] "Public entity" is defined as state and local governments, any department or other instrumentality of a state or local government, and certain transportation authorities. Thus, emergency services operated by a state or local government cannot discriminate against individuals with disabilities. Title III provides that no individual shall be discriminated against on the basis of disability in the full and equal enjoyment of the goods, services, facilities, privileges, advantages, or accommodations of any place of public accommodation by any person who owns, leases (or leases to), or operates a place of public accommodation.[9] Entities that are covered by the term "public accommodation" are listed in the statute and include, among others, hotels, restaurants, theaters, museums, parks, zoos, private schools, day care centers, professional offices of health-care providers, and gymnasiums.[10]

The ADA regulations do not specifically discuss emergencies but their general prohibitions against discrimination have been interpreted by the Department of Justice to apply to such situations.[11] However, recent changes to the regulations for titles II and III do contain a reference to emergencies in the provisions relating to communication.[12] Although generally, a public entity or a place of public accommodation may not require an individual to bring another individual to interpret for them,[13] there is an exception made for an "emergency involving an imminent threat to the safety or welfare of an individual or the public where there is no interpreter available."[14]

Department of Justice Guide

The Department of Justice has observed that "one of the most important roles of local government is to protect their citizenry from harm, including helping people prepare for and respond to emergencies. Making local government emergency preparedness and response programs accessible to people with disabilities is critical part of this responsibility. Making these programs accessible is also required by the ADA."[15]

The Department of Justice has issued an ADA guide for local governments regarding making community emergency preparedness and response programs accessible to people with disabilities.[16] This guide provides action steps, including

- planning for emergencies by soliciting and incorporating input from people with different types of disabilities for all phases of emergency plans;
- notification for individuals with disabilities when there is an emergency (e.g., providing ways to inform people who are deaf or hard of hearing of an impeding disaster);
- evacuation of individuals with disabilities (e.g., adopting policies to ensure community evacuation plans enable individuals with disabilities to safely self-evacuate or to be evacuated);
- sheltering of individuals with disabilities (surveying shelters and remove barriers, invite representatives of group homes and other individuals with disabilities to meet regarding shelter planning, adopting procedures to ensure individuals with disabilities are not separated from their service animals, ensuring that a reasonable number of emergency shelters have back-up generators and a way to keep medications refrigerated, and adopting procedures to provide accessible communication for people who are deaf or hard of hearing);
- issues involved in returning individuals with disabilities to their homes (arrange for accessible housing if necessary); and
- making sure that contracts for emergency services require providers to follow the guide's action steps.

FEMA Guidance

Title III of the ADA prohibits discrimination against individuals with disabilities in public accommodations. This prohibition in part requires that physical facilities be accessible if they are newly constructed or altered in a manner that affects the usability of the facility.[17] Any public accommodations that are rebuilt or significantly altered as a result of damage during a disaster must comply with the ADA's requirements for accessibility. Similarly, facilities that are rebuilt by states and localities (covered by Title II of the ADA) must also comply with the ADA's requirements for accessibility.[18]

The Federal Emergency Management Agency (FEMA) issued guidance in 2010 on planning for functional needs support services (FNSS) that can be incorporated into existing shelter plans by state emergency planners.[19] Generally, the guidance notes that "[c]hildren and adults with disabilities have the same right to services in general population shelters as other residents." In addition, planning must ensure that the shelters are accessible.[20] FNSS is defined as including

- reasonable modification to policies, practices and procedures;
- durable medical equipment;
- consumable medical supplies;
- personal assistance services; and
- other goods and services as needed.[21]

The legal authority for these requirements includes the ADA, Section 504 of the Rehabilitation Act of 1973,[22] and the Fair Housing Act.[23]

FEMA also issued guidance on October 26, 2000, for determining the eligibility of costs for federally required ADA access compliance associated with Public Assistance (PA) grants.[24] The PA program authorizes FEMA to fund the cost of repairing or replacing a public or private nonprofit facility. The ADA guidance provides that a new facility receiving FEMA funding and constructed as a replacement facility must be designed and constructed to be readily accessible to and usable by individuals with disabilities. Similarly, when ADA-relevant repairs are made to any area of an existing facility, they must be done to meet the needs of individuals with disabilities. FEMA will fund compliance with "reasonable ADA requirements in a new facility" and fund ADA relevant repairs to existing facilities with certain limitations. For example, funding for providing an accessible path of travel to a repaired area may not exceed 20% of the total cost associated with the repair of the primary function area. It should also be noted that some states and localities have imposed additional accessibility standards. FEMA notes that costs of additional state and local requirements may be eligible on a case-by-case basis if they are found reasonable.

NATIONWIDE PLAN REVIEW PHASE 2 REPORT

The Conference Report on the DHS Appropriations Act of 2006 directed the Secretary of DHS to report on the status of catastrophic planning in all 50 states and the nation's 75 largest urban areas.[25] DHS issued its report on June 16, 2006, and included a section on "special needs" populations. The term "special needs" is defined as including individuals with disabilities but also covers other groups such as children.[26] The report concluded that although progress was being made, "substantial improvement is necessary to integrate people with disabilities in emergency planning and readiness."[27] The report found that few plans recognized the legal obligations imposed by the ADA. Specific problems were identified regarding evacuation and transportation, communication and emergency public information, and sheltering and health services.[28]

EXECUTIVE ORDER 13347

President Bush issued Executive Order 13347, "Individuals with Disabilities in Emergency Preparedness," on July 22, 2004.[29] This executive order states that its policy is "to ensure that the Federal Government appropriately supports safety and security for individuals with disabilities in situations involving disasters, including earthquakes, tornadoes, fires, floods, hurricanes, and acts of terrorism...." Federal agencies are to consider the needs of individuals with disabilities in their emergency plans; to encourage this consideration in state, local, and tribal governments and private organization emergency planning; and to facilitate cooperation among federal, state, local, and tribal governments and private organizations. The Executive Order also established the Interagency Coordinating Council on Emergency Preparedness and Individuals with Disabilities (ICC) within DHS, which coordinates the implementation of the policies and submits an annual report. The annual report for 2005[30] noted several highlights from the ICC's work, including the creation of a disability preparedness resources center website,[31] new guidance on the ADA's requirements, workplace emergency preparedness guidelines for federal emergency planners, and an emergency transportation website.[32] The Emergency Preparedness in the Workplace Subcommittee of the ICC issued a report that provides guidelines for emergency plans for federal agencies. This report is meant to serve as a starting point for federal agencies as they reevaluate and strengthen their Occupant Emergency Plans (OEPs).[33]

POST-KATRINA EMERGENCY MANAGEMENT REFORM ACT OF 2006

The Post-Katrina Emergency Management Reform Act of 2006 added the position of disability coordinator to FEMA.[34] The disability coordinator reports directly to the Administrator of FEMA "to ensure that the needs of individuals with disabilities are being properly addressed in emergency preparedness and disaster relief."[35] The act contains a detailed list of the responsibilities of the Coordinator, which include providing guidance and coordination on matters related to individuals with disabilities in emergency planning and disaster relief, as well as interacting with the staff of FEMA, the National Council on Disability (NCD), the Interagency Coordinating Council on Preparedness and Individuals with Disabilities, and other federal, state, local, and tribal government entities. During congressional testimony in 2010, the current disability coordinator noted that the Office of Disability Integration and Coordination was established in FEMA in February 2010 and detailed some of the recent activities of the office. These included regular meetings with the

National Council on Disability, the National Council on Independent Living, and the DHS Office for Civil Rights and Civil Liberties; technical assistance; and training.[36]

The National Council on Disability has recommended that similar disability coordinator positions be created in regional FEMA offices to "enhance the effectiveness of the national disability coordinator by addressing more localized disability issues."[37] Legislation was introduced in the 111th Congress, S. 1386, which would have established an office of disability coordination in FEMA and regional disability coordinators.[38] The current disability coordinator testified that currently the staffing decisions rest in the regional FEMA offices and that most of them have chosen to incorporate the tasks of a disability coordinator into positions that already exist and work with individuals on disaster assistance.[39]

NATIONAL COUNCIL ON DISABILITY

The National Council on Disability (NCD), an independent federal agency responsible for gathering information on the development and implementation of federal laws, policies, programs, and initiatives that affect individuals with disabilities, issued several reports on emergency preparation and disaster relief relating to individuals with disabilities.[40] The most recent NCD report, "Effective Emergency Management: Making Improvements for Communities and People with Disabilities," evaluates emergency preparedness, disaster relief, and homeland security programs in the public and private sectors. It also provides examples of community efforts and offers recommendations. These recommendations include

- ensuring that disaster preparedness policies protect and maintain the independence of individuals with disabilities;
- requiring federal agencies to include disability organizations as partners in preparedness and outreach efforts;
- providing for alternative warning systems; and
- making shelters accessible.

John Vaughn, then NCD chairperson, testified before the Subcommittee on Economic Development, Public Buildings, and Emergency Management of the House Transportation and Infrastructure Committee regarding this report.[41] The principles of this report were also emphasized by the current chairperson of the NCD, Jonathan M. Young, in his testimony before the Subcommittee on Emergency Communications, Preparedness, and Response of the House Homeland Security Committee on June 15, 2010.[42] In addition, the Congressional Bipartisan Disabilities Caucus, the NCD, and the National Organization on Disability, among others, held a congressional briefing on November 10, 2005, entitled "Emergency Management and People with Disabilities: Before, During and After." This briefing included discussions of responsibilities for emergency management, disaster planning, and rebuilding, as well as other issues.[43]

End Notes

[1] http://www.census.gov/newsroom/releases/archives/income_wealth/cb08-185.html.

[2] For a discussion of disaster related issues, CRS Report RL34758, *The National Response Framework: Overview and Possible Issues for Congress*, by Bruce R. Lindsay; CRS Report RL33579, *The Public Health and Medical Response to Disasters: Federal Authority and Funding*, by Sarah A. Lister; and CRS Report R40159, *Public Health and Medical Preparedness and Response: Issues in the 111th Congress*, by Sarah A. Lister. Although it is beyond the scope of this report to discuss financial assistance provided to individuals with disabilities, it should be noted that P.L. 109-82, the Assistance for Individuals with Disabilities Affected by Hurricane Katrina or Rita Act of 2005, provides for certain reallotments of grants under the Rehabilitation Act of 1973 to assist individuals with disabilities affected by these disasters.

[3] 42 U.S.C. §12101 et seq.

[4] 42 U.S.C. §12101(b)(1). For a more detailed discussion of the ADA, see CRS Report 98-921, *The Americans with Disabilities Act (ADA): Statutory Language and Recent Issues*, by Nancy Lee Jones.

[5] P.L. 110-325, §4(a), amending 42 U.S.C. § 12102(3).

[6] See CRS Report RL34691, *The ADA Amendments Act: P.L. 110-325*, by Nancy Lee Jones.

[7] 42 U.S.C. §12112(a).

[8] 42 U.S.C. §§12131-12133.

[9] 42 U.S.C. §12182.

[10] 42 U.S.C. §12181.

[11] 28 C.F.R. Parts 35 (public entities) and 36 (places of public accommodation) (2010); 29 C.F.R. Part 1630 (employment)(2010).

[12] For a discussion of the changes made to the regulations see CRS Report R41376, *The Americans with Disabilities Act (ADA): Final Rule Amending Title II and Title III Regulations*, by Nancy Lee Jones.

[13] 28 C.F.R. §35.160(c)(2010); 28 C. F. R. §36.303(c)(2010).

[14] 28 C.F.R. §35.160(c)(2)(1)(2010); 28 C. F. R. §36.303(c)(3)(i)(2010).

[15] See http://www.usdoj.gov/crt/ada/emergencyprep.htm. This requirement would be under Title II of the ADA, which covers state and local governments.

[16] *Id.*

[17] 42 U.S.C. §12183; 28 C.F.R. §§36-401—36.407.

[18] 42 U.S.C. §12132; 28 C.F.R. §§35.149—35.151.

[19] http://www.fema.gov/pdf/about/odic/fnss_guidance.pdf.

[20] *Id.* at 8.

[21] *Id.*

[22] 29 U.S.C. §794. For a general discussion of section 504 see CRS Report RL34041, *Section 504 of the Rehabilitation Act of 1973: Prohibiting Discrimination Against Individuals with Disabilities in Programs or Activities Receiving Federal Assistance*, by Nancy Lee Jones.

[23] 42 U.S.C. §3601 et seq. For a general discussion of the Fair Housing Act see CRS Report 95-710, *The Fair Housing Act (FHA): A Legal Overview*, by Todd Garvey.

[24] See http://www.fema.gov/government/grant/pa/9525_5.shtm. This Stafford Act program authorizes FEMA to fund the cost of repairing, restoring, reconstructing, or replacing a public or private nonprofit facility in conformance with applicable codes, specifications and standards. 42 U.S.C. §5172(a). See also FEMA general standards (42 U.S.C. §5165a) and eligible cost considerations (42 U.S.C. §5172(e)).

[25] H.Rept. 109-241, 109th Cong., 1st Sess. (2005).

[26] The use of the term "special needs" has been criticized as limiting an integrated approach to emergency planning. See "Caring for Special Needs During Disasters: What's Being Done for Vulnerable Populations?" Hearing before the Subcommittee on Emergency Communications, Preparedness, and Response, House Homeland Security Committee, 111th Cong., 2d Sess. (June 15, 2010), (Testimony of Jonathan M. Young, Chairman, National Council on Disability) http://homeland.house.gov/SiteDocuments/20100615101428-34995.pdf; (Testimony of Marcie Roth, Director, Office of Disability Integration and Coordination, FEMA) http://homeland.house.gov/SiteDocuments/20100615101354-11995.pdf.

[27] U.S. Department of Homeland Security, *Nationwide Plan Review Phase 2 Report* 41 (June 16, 2006) at http://homelandsecurity.tamu.edu/framework/statelocalgovt/nationwide-plan-review-phase-2-report.html/. See also "Assessing the Impact of Hurricane Katrina on Persons with Disabilities" (January 2007), at http://www.rtcil.org/ products/NIDRR_FinalKatrinaReport.pdf.

[28] *Id.* at 46-47.

[29] See http://www.whitehouse.gov/news/releases/2004/07/20040722-10.html. In his statement on the 14th anniversary of the ADA in 2004, President Bush noted this executive order as one of the ways the administration had worked to foster the goals of the ADA. See http://www.whitehouse.gov/news/releases/2004/07/20040726-5.html.

[30] See http://www.dhs.gov/xlibrary/assets/CRCL_IWDEP_AnnualReport_2005.pdf.

[31] See http://www.dhs.gov/disabilitypreparedness.

[32] See http://www.dotcr.ost.dot.gov/asp/emergencyprep.asp.

[33] Interagency Coordinating Council on Emergency Preparedness and Individuals with Disabilities, Subcommittee on Emergency Preparedness in the Workplace, *A Framework of Emergency Preparedness Guidelines for Federal Agencies*, at http://www.dol.gov/odep/pubs/ep/preparing.htm. It should be noted that the ADA does not cover the executive branch or the U.S. Postal Service; these entities are covered by section 504 of the Rehabilitation Act of 1973, 29 U.S.C. §794, which provides similar protections.

[34] Section 513, of P.L. 109-295, 6 U.S.C. §321b.

[35] 6 U.S.C. §321b(a).

[36] Testimony of Marcie Roth, Director, Office of Disability Integration and Coordination, FEMA) http://homeland.house.gov/SiteDocuments/20100615101354-11995.pdf. The coordination with the National Council on Disability appears to address the concerns expressed by a GAO report which found that FEMA "has generally not coordinated with NCD as required by the Act, which could result in disability-related concerns not being fully addressed." Government Accountability Office, "National Disaster Response; FEMA Should Take Action to Improve Capacity and Coordination between Government and Voluntary Sectors," GAO-08-369 (Feb. 2008).

[37] National Council on Disability, "Effective Emergency Management: Making Improvements for Communities and People with Disabilities," at 336, http://www.ncd.gov/newsroom/publications/2009/pdf/ NCD_Emergency Management.pdf.

[38] Support for regional disability coordinators was also expressed at House hearings. "Caring for Special Needs During Disasters: What's Being Done for Vulnerable Populations?" Hearing before the Subcommittee on Emergency Communications, Preparedness, and Response, House Homeland Security Committee, 111th Cong., 2d Sess. (June 15, 2010), http://homeland.house.gov/SiteDocuments/20100615101320-72371.pdf.

[39] Testimony of Marcie Roth, Director, Office of Disability Integration and Coordination, FEMA) http://homeland.house.gov/SiteDocuments/20100615101354-11995.pdf.

[40] See http://www.ncd.gov/newsroom/publications/2009/pdf/NCD_EmergencyManagement.pdf; http://www. ncd.gov/ newsroom/publications/2005/saving_lives.htm; http://www.ncd.gov/newsroom/publications/2006/ hurricanes_impact.htm

[41] "Looking out for the Very Young, the Elderly and Others with Special Needs: Lessons from Katrina and other Major Disasters," Hearing before the Subcommittee on Economic Development, Public Buildings, and Emergency Management of the House Transportation and Infrastructure Committee, 111th Cong., 1st Sess. (October 19, 2009), http://transportation.

[42] "Caring for Special Needs During Disasters: What's Being Done for Vulnerable Populations?" Hearing before the Subcommittee on Emergency Communications, Preparedness, and Response, House Homeland Security Committee, 111th Cong., 2d Sess. (June 15, 2010), (Testimony of Jonathan M. Young, Chairman, National Council on Disability) http://homeland.house.gov/SiteDocuments/20100615101428-34995.pdf.

[43] For a transcript of this briefing, see http://www.ncd.gov/newsroom/publications /2005/transcript_emergencymgt.htm.

In: The Americans with Disabilities Act (ADA): Provisions…   ISBN: 978-1-61470-961-9
Editor: John Kiviniemi and Cécile Sanjo   © 2012 Nova Science Publishers, Inc.

Chapter 7

AMERICANS WITH DISABILITIES ACT (ADA) REQUIREMENTS CONCERNING THE PROVISION OF INTERPRETERS BY HOSPITALS AND DOCTORS

Nancy Lee Jones

SUMMARY

The Americans with Disabilities Act (ADA) is a broad civil rights act prohibiting discrimination against individuals with disabilities. Title III of the Americans with Disabilities Act (ADA) prohibits places of public accommodation, including hospitals and doctors' offices, from discriminating against individuals with disabilities. The Department of Justice (DOJ) promulgated regulations under title III requiring the use of auxiliary aids, unless they would fundamentally alter the nature of the service or result in an undue burden. Auxiliary aids may include qualified interpreters as well as note takers, video remote interpreting (VRI) services, or real-time computer-aided transcription services. The new regulations issued under title III on July 26, 2010, address several issues including the application of rights to effective communication by companions who are individuals with disabilities, the use of video remote interpreting (VRI) services, and when an accompanying adult or child may be used as an interpreter.

Attempting to address the myriad of disabilities and public accommodations, the ADA purposely adopted a flexible standard concerning when its nondiscrimination requirements are met. The law and DOJ regulations, then, do not explicitly state when hospitals or doctors are required to provide interpreter services to patients with disabilities and, as is illustrated by the judicial decisions in the area, this issue is largely fact dependent.

INTRODUCTION

The Americans with Disabilities Act (ADA) is a broad civil rights act prohibiting discrimination against individuals with disabilities.[1] Under title III of the ADA, discrimination against individuals with disabilities in public accommodations, including hospitals and doctor's offices, is prohibited.[2] The Department of Justice (DOJ) promulgated regulations under title III requiring places of public accommodation to provide "auxiliary aids and services" to individuals with disabilities unless they are able to prove such services would be unduly burdensome.[3] Auxiliary aids may include qualified interpreters as well as note takers, video remote interpreting (VRI) services, or real-time computer-aided transcription services.[4] The new regulations issued under title III on July 26, 2010, address several issues including the application of rights to effective communication by companions who are individuals with disabilities, the use of video remote interpreting (VRI) services, and when an accompanying adult or child may be used as an interpreter.

The auxiliary aid requirement articulated by the DOJ interprets the broad nondiscrimination language of the ADA and requires effective communication, but neither the statute nor the regulations explicitly state when doctors or hospitals must provide hearing impaired patients with interpreters. As a result, the answer as to whether doctors or hospitals must provide interpreters for hearing impaired individuals is dependent on the particular circumstances surrounding the patient's case. Judicial decisions give some guidance on when an interpreter must be provided in particular factual situations.

STATUTORY LANGUAGE

Title III of the ADA provides that "[n]o individual shall be discriminated against on the basis of disability in the full and equal enjoyment of the goods, services, facilities, privileges, advantages, or accommodations of any place of public accommodation by any person who owns, leases (or leases to), or operates a place of public accommodation."[5] Discrimination is further described as including "a failure to make reasonable modifications in policies, practices, or procedures when such modifications are necessary to afford such goods, services, facilities, privileges, advantages, or accommodations to individuals with disabilities."[6] Public accommodations are exempted from providing these special provisions when they "can demonstrate that making such modification would fundamentally alter the nature of such goods, services, facilities, privileges, advantages, or accommodations."[7] The definition of public accommodation specifically includes the "professional office of a health care professional" and hospitals.[8]

REGULATORY INTERPRETATION AND GUIDANCE

On July 26, 2010, the 20th anniversary of the passage of the ADA, the Department of Justice (DOJ) issued final rules amending the existing regulations under ADA title II (prohibiting discrimination against individuals with disabilities by state and local governments) and ADA title III (prohibiting discrimination against individuals with disabilities by places of public accommodations).[9] These new regulations contain detailed sections on communications. Like the previous regulations, the new regulations require that public entities and public accommodations furnish appropriate aids and services when necessary to ensure effective communication with an exception regarding fundamental alterations or undue burdens. More specifically, the title III regulations state that public accommodations do not have to provide auxiliary aids if such measures would "fundamentally alter the nature of the goods, services, facilities, privileges, advantages, or accommodations being offered or would result in an undue burden, i.e., significant difficulty or expense."[10] In determining whether an action poses an undue burden, the regulations require the consideration of several factors, including the nature and cost of the action, the overall financial resources of the site, the geographic separateness and the administrative or fiscal relationship of the site or sites in question to a parent corporation, the overall financial resources of the parent corporation, and the type of operation or operations of any parent corporation or entity.[11] When a particular auxiliary aid would cause an undue burden, the public accommodation must provide alternative assistance so that the individual can take full advantage of the services and goods offered.[12]

Unlike the previous regulations, the new regulations specifically extend the requirement for effective communication to companions who are individuals with disabilities. DOJ noted in its comments on the new regulations that this was a particularly important issue.

Effective communication with companions is particularly critical in health care settings where miscommunication may lead to misdiagnosis and improper or delayed medical treatment. The Department has encountered confusion and reluctance by medical care providers regarding the scope of their obligation with respect to such companions. Effective communication with a companion is necessary in a variety of circumstances. For example, a companion may be authorized to make health care decision on behalf of the patient or may need to help the patient with information or instructions given by hospital personnel. A companion may be the patient's next-of-kin or health care surrogate with whom the hospital must communicate about the patient's medical condition.[13]

The new regulations also indicate that the type of auxiliary aid or service necessary for effective communication varies depending on the circumstance.[14] The new title III regulations specifically state that "[a] public accommodation should consult with individuals with disabilities whenever possible to determine what type of auxiliary aid is needed to ensure effective communication, but the ultimate decision as to what measure to take rests with the public accommodation, provided that the method chosen results in effective communication."[15]

The term "auxiliary aid" is defined to include "qualified interpreters on site or through video remote interpreting (VRI) services, notetakers, real-time computer-aided transcription services, written materials; exchange of written notes ... or other effective methods of making aurally delivered materials available to individuals who are deaf or hard of hearing."[16] The new regulations added video remote services (VRI) as an example of an auxiliary aid that may provide effective communication.[17] The new regulations specifically state that when VRI is used it must provide

- real-time, full-motion video and audio over a dedicated high-speed, wide-bandwidth video or wireless connection that does not produce lags, choppy, blurry or grainy images or irregular pauses in communications;

- a sharply delineated image that is large enough to display the interpreter's face, arms, hands, and fingers and the participating individual's face, arms, hands, and fingers; and
- a clear, audible transmission of voices.

In addition, a public accommodation that uses VRI must provide adequate training to users of the technology and other involved individuals.[18]

The new regulations also discuss when a family member or a friend may be used as an interpreter. Generally, a public accommodation is not to rely on an adult who accompanies an individual with a disability to interpret for the individual.[19] However, there are some exceptions including an emergency involving an imminent threat to safety or welfare, and where the individual with a disability specifically requests that the accompanying adult interpret and the accompanying adult agrees.[20] A minor child may not be used to interpret except in an emergency situation.[21]

JUDICIAL INTERPRETATION

Effective Communication

As the regulations indicate, there is no absolute requirement that an interpreter be provided in a particular situation. However, in order to comply with the ADA, auxiliary aids must provide effective doctor-patient communication. In *Mayberry v. Van Valtier,* the court held that a deaf Medicare patient was entitled to a trial on her claim that her doctor violated the ADA.[22] In this case, the doctor had communicated with the patient for several years mostly by exchanging notes or using the patient's children as sign interpreters and on one occasion had noted in the patient's file that her back pain was higher than she had originally thought and that this misunderstanding was "probably due to poor communication." The patient, Mrs. Mayberry, requested that the doctor provide an interpreter for a physical examination. The doctor complied but following the examination wrote a letter to the interpreter, with a copy to the patient, stating that she would not be able to use the interpreter's services again and that "I really can't afford to take care of Mrs. Mayberry at all." The doctor characterized the letter as a protest against what was perceived as an unfair law. The court found that the allegations made by the patient were sufficient to reject a motion for summary judgment and ordered the case to proceed to trial. Subsequently, a judgment was rendered in favor of the doctor but there is no record of a written opinion.[23]

In *Aikins v. St. Helena Hospital*, another district court examined arguments concerning effective communication and denied summary judgment to the hospital and doctor.[24] Elaine Aikins, a hearing impaired individual, and the California Association of the Deaf (CAD) alleged that St. Helena Hospital and Dr. James Lies failed to communicate effectively with Mrs. Aikins during her now deceased husband's medical treatment. Instead of an interpreter, the hospital provided Mrs. Aikins with an ineffective finger speller. Allegedly Mrs. Aikins was unable to effectively communicate with Dr. Lies or other hospital staff until her daughter became available to interpret, an argument that was supported by the doctor's mistaken impression concerning how long the patient had been without CPR. Mrs. Aikins and the CAD alleged that Dr. Lies and St. Helena Hospital violated both the ADA and the Rehabilitation Act. Dr. Lies maintained that the Rehabilitation Act was inapplicable and St. Helena asserted that it complied with both the ADA and Rehabilitation Act. Although the ADA claims were dismissed due to lack of standing, the court noted that adequate medical treatment is not a defense to a claim that a defendant failed to provide effective communication under the Rehabilitation Act of 1973.[25] "Mrs. Aikins's claims relate to her exclusion from meaningful participation in the decisions affecting her husband's treatment, not to the appropriateness of the treatment itself."[26]

Citing *Aikins*, the court in *Naiman v. New York University* found that a physician's effectiveness in providing medical treatment to a hearing impaired patient does not negate an ineffective communication claim under the ADA.[27] Mr. Alec Naiman, who is hearing impaired, was admitted on several occasions to New York University Medical Center, one of many medical facilities operated by New York University. On each occasion Mr. Naiman requested an interpreter in order to "effectively participate in his treatment" and communicate with hospital staff. With the exception of one visit, the center failed to provide one in a timely manner or did not provide an interpreter at all. New York University argued that Mr. Naiman failed to state a claim under the ADA because he received adequate medical care from the medical center. The court disagreed and ruled in favor of the plaintiff. The court noted that an effective communication claim under the ADA relates to the patient's exclusion from participation in his treatment rather than the treatment itself. Therefore, the effectiveness of the treatment is an insufficient defense to the general purpose and scope of the ADA.[28]

As DOJ discussed in its appendix to the ADA Title III regulations, although physicians and hospitals are strongly encouraged to confer with patients with disabilities about the type of auxiliary aid they prefer when communicating, deference to the patient's preferred method is not necessarily required. In *Majocha v. Turner*, the district court denied a motion for summary judgment in a case involving the lack of an interpreter for the father of a 15-month-old patient.[29] The defendant doctors argued that they had offered to use note taking to communicate. The district court observed that an individual with a disability cannot insist on a particular auxiliary aid if the aid offered ensures effective communication. However, the court, relying on lay and expert testimony concerning the lack of effectiveness of note taking in this case, found that there was a genuine dispute regarding whether the note taking was an acceptable auxiliary aid and denied the doctors' motion for summary judgment.[30]

Undue Burden

The law provides that an interpreter, or any suggested auxiliary aid, is not required if the doctor can demonstrate that doing so would "fundamentally alter the nature of the good, services, facility, privilege, advantage, or accommodation being offered or would result in an undue burden."[31] This issue was discussed in *Bravin v. Mount Sinai Medical Center,* where the plaintiff sued a hospital for failure to provide a sign language interpreter during a Lamaze class.[32] The court there found that while the hospital alluded to undue hardship, it did not address the issue explicitly. Therefore, because there was no issue of fact as to whether the hospital violated the ADA, the court awarded summary judgment to the plaintiff.[33]

The Senate report on the ADA noted that "technological advances can be expected to further enhance options for making meaningful and effective opportunities available to individuals with disabilities. Such advances may enable covered entities to provide auxiliary aids and services which today might be considered to impose undue burdens on such entities."[34] Recently, videoconferencing technology, combined with high-speed internet connections, has been used to provide around-the-clock interpreting services for businesses.[35] Additionally, the use of CART technology has been employed as a means to efficiently communicate with hearing impaired individuals.[36] This may render successful undue burden arguments increasingly difficult. However, the use of technology must result in effective communication.[37]

Deliberate Indifference

Several cases have held that to establish a claim for damages, a plaintiff must show that a defendant is guilty of intentional discrimination or deliberate indifference. In *Loeffler v. Staten Island University Hospital,*[38] a case brought under Section 504 of the Rehabilitation Act,[39] the Second Circuit Court of Appeals held the factual situation could support a finding of deliberate indifference. Robert Loeffler and his wife were deaf but their two children, ages 13 and 17, had normal hearing. The Loefflers stated that prior to Mr. Loeffler's heart surgery, they requested an interpreter but one was never furnished and their children served as translators, even in the surgery recovery room and the critical care unit.

Several plaintiffs have argued that defendant hospitals have shown deliberate indifference when a sign language interpreter was requested but not provided. In *Freydel v. New York Hospital,* the court of appeals found that the hospital had a policy to provide interpreter services and had attempted to secure an interpreter for a 78 year old deaf woman who communicated in Russian sign language.[40] The second circuit held that proving that staff members failed to respond to repeated requests for a Russian sign language interpreter "cannot by itself suffice to maintain a claim of deliberate indifference." Similarly, in *Constance v. State University of New York Health Science Center,* the court denied the plaintiffs' motion for damages finding that the hospital responded quickly to a request for an interpreter.[41] Although the failure to follow up on the request may have been negligent, the court found it did not amount to deliberate indifference. In *Alvarez v. New York City Health & Hospitals Corporation,*[42] the district court reached a similar conclusion, finding that the plaintiff did not make the required showing of deliberate indifference since the hospital has a policy of providing interpreters and provided an interpreter within a day of the request.

Standing

One of the threshold issues a plaintiff must overcome before the merits of a case can be examined is whether the plaintiff has standing to bring an ADA claim.[43] Several decisions have found that a plaintiff who alleges discrimination under the ADA due to lack of a sign language interpreter does not have standing because there is not a real and immediate threat of harm.[44] However, other decisions have found standing. For example, in *Gillespie v. Dimensions Health Corporation,* the district court found standing for plaintiffs alleging "the existing and on-going policy and practice [of not providing interpreters] itself violates their rights under the ADA."[45] In addition, because the plaintiffs had sought, and would likely continue to seek, medical care from the hospital, there was a sufficient threat of future ADA violations to grant the plaintiffs standing under the ADA.[46]

ANALYSIS AND CONCLUSION

The ADA purposely adopted a flexible standard regarding nondiscrimination requirements. This flexibility was seen as a means to balance the rights of the patients with disabilities the interests of treating physicians and hospitals. Because of this flexibility, precise requirements are not readily enunciated. Therefore, whether or not a doctor or hospital must provide an interpreter for a hearing impaired individual depends on the particular circumstances surrounding the patient's care.[47]

Exactly when a sign language interpreter may be required has been discussed in several judicial decisions. However, the majority of the claims regarding the failure of a doctor to provide a hearing impaired patient with an interpreter appear to have been resolved through either an informal or formal settlement process. The DOJ has obtained a number of settlement agreements with hospitals in recent years.[48] In addition, the new regulations promulgated under title III address several issues including the application of rights to effective communication by companions who are individuals with disabilities, a specific discussion of the use of video remote interpreting (VRI) services, and when an accompanying adult or child may be used as an interpreter.[49]

End Notes

[1] 42 U.S.C. §§12101 et seq. For a more detailed discussion of the ADA, see CRS Report 98-921, *The Americans with Disabilities Act (ADA): Statutory Language and Recent Issues*, by Nancy Lee Jones.

[2] 42 U.S.C. §12182.

[3] 28 C.F.R. §36.303.

[4] 28 C.F.R. §36.303(b).

[5] 42 U.S.C. §12182. Section 504 of the Rehabilitation Act, 29 U.S.C. §794, prohibits discrimination against individuals with disabilities in any program or activity that receives federal financial assistance, and the requirements of the ADA and Section 504 are generally interpreted in the same manner. For a more detailed discussion of Section 504 see CRS Report RL34041, *Section 504 of the Rehabilitation Act of 1973: Prohibiting Discrimination Against Individuals with Disabilities in Programs or Activities Receiving Federal Assistance*, by Nancy Lee Jones.

[6] 42 U.S.C. §12182.

[7] *Id.*

[8] 42 U.S.C. §12181(7)(F).

[9] http://www.ada.gov/regs2010/ADAregs2010.htm. The following discussion centers on the title III regulations since they are most applicable to hospitals and doctors' offices. For a discussion of the major changes made to both title II and title III regulations see CRS Report R41376, *The Americans with Disabilities Act (ADA): Final Rule Amending Title II and Title III Regulations*, by Nancy Lee Jones.

[10] 28 C.F.R. §36.303(a).

[11] 28 C.F.R. §36.104.

[12] 28 C.F.R. §36.303(g).

[13] 28 C.F.R. §35.160(a)(2)(title II); 28 C.F.R. §36.303 (title III).

[14] 28 C.F.R. §35.160(b)(2)(title II); 28 C.F.R. §36.303(c) (title III).

[15] 28 C.F.R. §36.303(c)(1)(ii).

[16] 28 C.F.R. §36.303(b)(1).

[17] VRI is defined in the regulations as "an interpreting service that uses video conference technology over dedicated lines or wireless technology offering high-speed, wide-bandwidth video connection or wireless connections that delivers high-quality video images...." 28 C.F.R. §36.104.

[18] 28 C.F.R. §36.303(f).

[19] 28 C.F.R. §36.303(c)(2).

[20] 28 C.F.R. §36.303(c)(3).

[21] 28 C.F.R. §36.303(c)(4).

[22] 843 F.Supp. 1160 (E.D. Mich. 1994).

[23] Eastern District, Michigan, Docket # 114 (May 22, 1995).

[24] 843 F.Supp. 1329 (N.D. Calif. 1994).

[25] The Rehabilitation Act of 1973 prohibits entities receiving federal funds from discriminating against individuals on the basis of a disability and is generally interpreted in the same manner as the ADA. 29 U.S.C. § 794(a).

[26] 843 F.Supp. 1329, 1338 (N.D. Calif. 1994).

[27] *Naiman v. New York University*, 1997 U.S. Dist LEXIS 6616 (S.D.N.Y. May 13, 1997).

[28] See Michael A. Schwartz, *Deaf Patients, Doctors, and the Law: Compelling A Conversation about Communication*, 35 Fla. St. L. Rev. 947, 970 (2008). Schwartz notes that the ADA is intended to ensure equal access to services rather than effective treatment. *Id.*

[29] 166 F.Supp.2d 316 (W.D. Pa. 2001).

[30] See also Naiman v. New York University, 1997 U.S. Dist. LEXIS 6616 (S.D.N.Y. May 13, 1997), where the court noted that it agreed with the hospital "that its obligation was to provide effective communication under the circumstances, and not necessarily a qualified interpreter as Naiman claims."

[31] 42 U.S.C. §12182(b)(2)(A)(iii); 28 C.F.R. § 36.303.

[32] 186 F.R.D. 293 (S.D. N.Y. 1999).

[33] The court granted a motion for reconsideration and vacated the summary judgment regarding the finding of intentional discrimination because genuine issues of fact existed as to whether the hospital acted with deliberate indifference. *Bravin v. Mount Sinai Medical Center*, 58 F.Supp. 2d 269 (S.D. N.Y. 1999).

[34] S. Rep. No. 101-116, 101st Cong., 1st Sess. (1989), reprinted in 1 Legislative History of P.L. 101-336, The Americans with Disabilities Act, Prepared for the House Committee on Education and Labor, Serial No. 102-A, pp. 162-163 (December 1990).

[35] See, e.g., http://www.deaf-talk.com/.

[36] CART technology, or "computer-aided real-time transcription," is a system where spoken word is instantly translated into text on a computer. For more information see http://www.cartinfo.org.

[37] See e.g., Gillespie v. Dimensions Health Corporation, 369 F.Supp.2d 636 (D. Md. 2005), where the Plaintiffs alleged that the video conferencing device was "wholly ineffective, either because the staff was inadequately trained and unable to operate the VRI device, because Plaintiffs were unable to understand the video interpreter due to the poor quality of the video transmission, or both."

[38] 582 F.3d 268 (2d Cir. 2009).

[39] 29 U.S.C. §794. Section 504 prohibits discrimination against individuals with disabilities in any program or activity that receives federal funds. Since the ADA was modeled on Section 504 of the Rehabilitation Act, courts generally interpret the requirements in the same manner.

[40] Freydel v. New York Hospital, 2000 U.S. App. LEXIS 31862 (2d Cir. 2000).

[41] Constance v. State University of New York Health Science Center, 166 F.Supp.2d 663 (N.D. N.Y. 2001).

[42] 2002 U.S. Dist LEXIS 12986 (S.D.N.Y. 2002).

[43] For a more detailed discussion of standing and the use of interpreters by hospitals and doctors see Michael A. Schwartz, "Limits on Injunctive Relief Under the ADA: Rethinking the Standing Rule for Deaf Patients in the Medical Setting," 11 J. of Health Care L. & Policy 163 (2008).

[44] See e.g. Aikins v. St. Helena Hospital, 843 F.Supp. 1329 (N.D. Cal. 1994); Proctor v. Prince George's Hosp. Ctr., 32 F.Supp.2d 820 (D. Md. 1998); Davis v. Flexman,109 F.Supp.2d 776 (S.D. Ohio 1999). See also Loeffler v. Staten Island University Hospital, 2007 U.S. Dist. LEXIS 22038 (E.D.N.Y. 2007),where the court found that the "mere fact that Josephine visited the Hospital a few times since 1995 does not constitute a 'real and immediate threat of repeated injury.'" *Id.* The *Loeffler* court also noted that the hospital had sufficiently amended its policy concerning interpreters to ensure that interpreters would be available when needed. *Id.*

[45] Gillespie v. Dimensions Health Corporation, 369 F.Supp.2d 636 (D.Md. 2005).

[46] See also Benavides v. Laredo Medical Center, 2009 U.S. Dist. LEXIS 51353 (S.D. Texas June 18, 2009), where the court found standing under Title III of the ADA since the plaintiff had stated that he suffered from conditions that are likely to require attention, the defendant's hospital was the closest to his home, and the hospital had denied requests for an interpreter three separate times.

[47] See, Department of Justice, Disability Rights Section of the Civil Rights Division, "Communicating with People who are Deaf or Hard of Hearing in Hospital Settings," http://www.ada.gov/hospcombr.htm.

[48] See e.g., http://www.usdoj.gov/crt/ada/devin.htm, http://www.usdoj.gov/crt/ada/davishos.htm, http://www.usdoj.gov/ crt/ada/stluke.htm, and http://www.usdoj.gov/crt/ada/shillhos.htm.

[49] http://www.ada.gov/regs2010/titleIII_2010/reg3_2010.html, 28 C.F.R. §36.303 (title III).

In: The Americans with Disabilities Act (ADA): Provisions...   ISBN: 978-1-61470-961-9
Editor: John Kiviniemi and Cécile Sanjo   © 2012 Nova Science Publishers, Inc.

Chapter 8

THE AMERICANS WITH DISABILITIES ACT (ADA) COVERAGE OF CONTAGIOUS DISEASES

Nancy Lee Jones

SUMMARY

The Americans with Disabilities Act (ADA), 42 U.S.C. §§12101 *et seq.,* provides broad nondiscrimination protection for individuals with disabilities in employment, public services, public accommodations and services operated by private entities, transportation, and telecommunications. As stated in the act, its purpose is "to provide a clear and comprehensive national mandate for the elimination of discrimination against individuals with disabilities." Due to concern about the spread of highly contagious diseases such as pandemic influenza and extensively drug-resistant tuberculosis (XDR-TB), questions have been raised about the application of the ADA in such situations. Generally, individuals with serious contagious diseases would most likely be considered individuals with disabilities. However, this does not mean that an individual with a serious contagious disease would have to be hired or given access to a place of public accommodation if such an action would place other individuals at a significant risk. Such determinations are highly fact specific and the differences between the contagious diseases may give rise to differing conclusions since each contagious disease has specific patterns of transmission that affect the magnitude and duration of a potential threat to others.

INTRODUCTION

The Americans with Disabilities Act, often described as the most sweeping nondiscrimination legislation since the Civil Rights Act of 1964, provides protections against discrimination for individuals with disabilities.[1] Due to concern about the spread of highly contagious diseases such as the 2009 H1N1 pandemic influenza[2] and extensively drug-resistant tuberculosis (XDR-TB),[3] questions have been raised about the application of the ADA in such situations. The threshold issue when discussing the applicability of the ADA is whether the individual in question is a person with a disability. Generally, individuals with serious contagious diseases would most likely be considered individuals with disabilities.[4] However, this does not mean that an individual with a serious contagious disease would have to be hired or given access to a place of public accommodation if such an action would place other individuals at a significant risk. Such determinations are highly fact specific and the differences between the contagious diseases discussed by the courts (e.g., HIV infection, tuberculosis, and hepatitis) and pandemic influenza may give rise to differing conclusions. Each contagious disease has specific patterns of transmission that affect the magnitude and duration of a potential threat to others.[5]

STATUTORY LANGUAGE AND LEGISLATIVE HISTORY

Definition of Disability

The starting point for an analysis of rights provided by the ADA is whether an individual is an individual with a disability. The term "disability," with respect to an individual, is defined as "(A) a physical or mental impairment that substantially limits one or more of the major life activities of such individual; (B) a record of such an impairment; or (C) being regarded as having such an impairment (as described in paragraph(3))."[6] The ADA was amended by the ADA Amendments Act of 2008, P.L. 110-325, to expand the interpretation of the definition of disability from that of several Supreme Court decisions.[7] Although the statutory language is essentially the same as it was in the original ADA, P.L. 110-325 contains new rules of construction regarding the definition of disability, which provide that

- the definition of disability shall be construed in favor of broad coverage to the maximum extent permitted by the terms of the act;
- the term "substantially limits" shall be interpreted consistently with the findings and purposes of the ADA Amendments Act;
- an impairment that substantially limits one major life activity need not limit other major life activities to be considered a disability;
- an impairment that is episodic or in remission is a disability if it would have substantially limited a major life activity when active;
- the determination of whether an impairment substantially limits a major life activity shall be made without regard to the ameliorative effects of mitigating measures, except that the ameliorative effects of ordinary eyeglasses or contact lenses shall be considered.[8]

Generally, individuals with serious contagious diseases would most likely be considered individuals with disabilities.[9] However, what is defined as a "serious" contagious disease is fact specific. For example, the Equal Employment Opportunity Commission (EEOC) has indicated that individuals infected with the 2009 H1N1 pandemic influenza virus would not be individuals with disabilities. However, if the disease were to become more severe, an infected individual might be considered to be an individual with a disability under the ADA.[10] The EEOC guidance does not delineate when the illness would be serious enough to be encompassed by the ADA. Even if a contagious disease is serious and an infected individual is covered by the ADA, if that individual poses a direct threat to others, he or she would not necessarily have to be hired or given access to a place of public accommodation.

Direct Threat

Title I of the ADA, which prohibits employment discrimination against otherwise qualified individuals with disabilities, specifically states that "the term 'qualifications standards' may include a requirement that an individual shall not pose a direct threat to the health or safety of other individuals in the workplace."[11] In addition, the Secretary of Health and Human Services (HHS) is required to publish, and update, a list of infectious and communicable diseases that may be transmitted through handling the food supply.[12] Similarly, title III, which prohibits discrimination in public accommodations and services operated by private entities, states: "Nothing in this title shall require an entity to permit an individual to participate in or benefit from the goods, services, facilities, privileges, advantages and accommodations of such entity where such individual poses a direct threat to the health or safety of others. The term 'direct threat' means a significant risk to the health or safety of others that cannot be eliminated by a modification of policies, practices, or procedures or by the provision of auxiliary aids or services."[13] Although title II, which prohibits discrimination by state and local government services, does not contain such specific language, it does require an individual to be "qualified" and this is defined in part as meeting "the essential eligibility requirements of the receipt of services or the participation in programs or activities...."[14]

Contagious diseases were discussed in the ADA's legislative history. The Senate report noted that the qualification standards permitted with regard to employment under title I may include a requirement that an individual with a currently contagious disease or infection shall not pose a direct threat to the health or safety of other individuals in the workplace and cited to *School Board of Nassau County v. Arline*,[15] a Supreme Court decision concerning contagious diseases and Section 504 of the Rehabilitation Act of 1973.[16] Similarly, the House report of the Committee on Education and Labor reiterated the reference to *Arline* and added "[t]hus the term 'direct threat' is meant to connote the full standard set forth in the *Arline* decision."[17]

ADA REGULATIONS

The Department of Justice issued amended regulations for titles II and III of the ADA which were published in the Federal Register on September 15, 2010.[18] Although these regulations did not directly address contagious diseases, they did contain some revised language concerning the direct threat exception. Both the title II and title III regulations provide that public entities or places of public accommodations are not required to permit an individual to participate in services or activities when that individual poses a direct threat to the health or safety of others.[19] In determining whether an individual poses a direct threat, both titles require "an individualized assessment, based on reasonable judgment that relies on current medical knowledge or on the best available objective evidence, to ascertain: The nature, duration, and severity of the risk; the probability that the potential injury will actually occur; and whether reasonable modifications of policies, practices, or procedures or the provision of auxiliary aids or services will mitigate the risk."[20]

SUPREME COURT DECISIONS

School Board of Nassau County v. Arline

Section 504 of the Rehabilitation Act of 1973, 29 U.S.C. §794, in part prohibits discrimination against an otherwise qualified individual with a disability in any program or activity that receives federal financial assistance. Many of the concepts used in the ADA originated in Section 504, its regulations, and judicial interpretations. The legislative history of the ADA, as discussed above, specifically cited to the Supreme Court's interpretation of Section 504 in *Arline* which held that a person with active tuberculosis was an individual with a disability but may not be otherwise qualified to teach elementary school. Footnote 16, which was referenced in the ADA's legislative history, states in relevant part that "a person who poses a significant risk of communicating an infectious disease to others in the workplace will not be otherwise qualified for his or her job if reasonable accommodation will not eliminate that risk."[21]

The Court in *Arline* examined the standards to be used to determine if an individual with a contagious disease is otherwise qualified. In most cases, the Court observed, an individualized inquiry is necessary in order to protect individuals with disabilities from "deprivation based on prejudice, stereotypes, or unfounded fear, while giving appropriate weight to such legitimate concerns of grantees as avoiding exposing others to significant health and safety risks."[22] The Court adopted the test enunciated by the American Medical Association (AMA) amicus brief and held that the factors which must be considered include "findings of facts, based on reasonable medical judgments given the state of medical knowledge, about (a) the nature of the risk (how the disease is transmitted), (b) the duration of the risk (how long is the carrier infectious), (c) the severity of the risk (what is the potential harm to third parties) and (d) the probabilities the disease will be transmitted and will cause varying degrees of harm."[23] The Court also emphasized that courts "normally should defer to the reasonable medical judgments of public health officials" and that courts must consider whether the employer could reasonably accommodate the employee.[24] *Arline* was remanded for consideration of the facts using this standard and the district court held that since the teacher had had negative cultures and the possibility of infection was "extremely rare," the school board must reinstate her or pay her salary until retirement eligibility.[25]

Bragdon v. Abbott

The Supreme Court in *Bragdon v. Abbott*,[26] addressed the ADA definition of individual with a disability and held that the respondent's asymptomatic HIV infection was a physical impairment impacting on the major life activity of reproduction thus rendering the HIV infection a disability under the ADA. The Court also addressed the question of what is a direct threat, finding that the ADA's direct threat language codified the Court's decision in *Arline*. In *Bragdon* the plaintiff, an individual with asymptomatic HIV infection, sought dental treatment from the defendant and was told that she would be treated only in a hospital, not in the office. The plaintiff, Ms. Abbott, filed an ADA complaint and prevailed at the district court, court of appeals and the Supreme Court on the issue of whether she was an individual with a disability but the case was remanded for further consideration regarding the issue of direct threat.

The Supreme Court provided some guidance regarding the direct threat issue in *Bragdon* stating that "the existence, or nonexistence, of a significant risk must be determined from the standpoint of the person who refuses the treatment or accommodation, and the risk assessment must be based on medical or other objective evidence." Dr. Bragdon had the duty to assess the risk of infection "based on the objective, scientific information available to him and others in his profession. His belief that a significant risk existed, even if maintained in good faith, would not relieve him from liability." On remand for consideration of the direct threat issue, the first circuit court of appeals held that summary judgment was warranted, finding that Dr. Bragdon's evidence was too speculative or too tangential to create a genuine issue of fact.[27]

Chevron U.S.A. Inc., v. Echazabal

Both *Arline* and *Bragdon* dealt with the issue of whether an individual was a direct threat to others. In *Chevron U.S.A. Inc., v. Echazabal*,[28] the Supreme Court dealt with the issue of whether an individual was a threat to himself and held unanimously that the ADA does not require an employer to hire an individual with a disability if the job in question would endanger that individual's health. The ADA's statutory language provides for a defense to an allegation of discrimination that a qualification standard is "job related and consistent with business necessity."[29] The act also allows an employer to impose as a qualification standard that the individual shall not pose a direct threat to the health or safety of other individuals in the workplace[30] but does not discuss a threat to the individual's health or safety. The ninth circuit in *Echazabal* had determined that an employer violated the ADA by refusing to hire an applicant with a serious liver condition whose illness would be aggravated through exposure to the chemicals in the workplace.[31] The Supreme Court rejected the ninth circuit decision and upheld a regulation by the EEOC that allows an employer to assert a direct threat defense to an allegation of employment discrimination where the threat is posed only to the health or safety of the individual making the allegation.[32] Justice Souter found that the EEOC regulations were not the kind of workplace paternalism that the ADA seeks to outlaw. "The EEOC was certainly acting within the reasonable zone when it saw a difference between rejecting workplace paternalism and ignoring specific and documented risks to the employee himself, even if the employee would take his chances for the sake of getting a job." The Court emphasized that a direct threat defense must be based on medical judgment that uses the most current medical knowledge.

LOWER COURT DECISIONS

The lower courts have dealt with a number of direct threat cases under the ADA. Although a comprehensive survey of these cases is beyond the scope of this report, they have involved a number of types of disabilities as well as varying occupations and accommodations. The disabilities at issue have often involved AIDS or HIV infection[33] or mental illness[34] but have also included hepatitis,[35] and other conditions. The various occupations have included public health care workers, public safety officers, transportation operators, food handlers, and industrial workers.[36]

End Notes

[1] For a more detailed discussion of the ADA see CRS Report 98-921, *The Americans with Disabilities Act (ADA): Statutory Language and Recent Issues*, by Nancy Lee Jones. Other federal statutes concerning the civil rights of individuals with disabilities also have interpreted issues relating to individuals with contagious diseases in a manner similar to the ADA. See *School Board of Nassau County v. Arline*, 480 U.S. 273 (1987), interpreting Section 504 of the Rehabilitation Act, 29 U.S.C. §794, and 14 C.F.R. §382.51 interpreting the Air Carriers Access Act. For a discussion of the Air Carriers Access Act, see CRS Report RL34047, *Overview of the Air Carrier Access Act (ACAA)*, by Emily C. Barbour.

[2] For a detailed discussion of the H1N1 influenza pandemic see CRS Report R40554, *The 2009 Influenza Pandemic: An Overview*, by Sarah A. Lister and C. Stephen Redhead; CRS Report R40560, *The 2009 Influenza Pandemic: Selected Legal Issues*, coordinated by Kathleen S. Swendiman and Nancy Lee Jones; and CRS Report R40866, *The Americans with Disabilities Act (ADA): Employment Issues and the 2009 Influenza Pandemic*, by Nancy Lee Jones.

[3] See CRS Report RL34144, *Extensively Drug-Resistant Tuberculosis (XDR-TB): Emerging Public Health Threats and Quarantine and Isolation*, by Kathleen S. Swendiman and Nancy Lee Jones.

[4] See *Bragdon v. Abbott*, 524 U.S. 624 (1998). The issues involving the definition of disability have been among the most controversial under the ADA. The ADA was amended to expand the interpretation of the definition of disability. See CRS Report RL34691, *The ADA Amendments Act: P.L. 110-325*, by Nancy Lee Jones.

[5] See David L. Heymann, *Control of Communicable Diseases Manual*, 18th ed., an official report of the American Public Health Association, 2004.

[6] 42 U.S.C. §12102(2) as amended by P.L. 110-325, §4(a).

[7] Sutton v. United Air Lines, Inc., 527 U.S. 471 (1999); Murphy v. United Parcel Service, Inc., 527 U.S. 516 (1999); Kirkingburg v. Albertson's Inc., 527 U.S. 555 (1999); Toyota Motor Manufacturing v. Williams, 534 U.S. 184 (2002). For a more detailed discussion of P.L. 110-325 see CRS Report RL34691, The ADA Amendments Act: P.L. 110-325, by Nancy Lee Jones.

[8] Low vision devices are not included in the ordinary eyeglasses and contact lens exception.

[9] See *Bragdon v. Abbott*, 524 U.S. 624 (1998), discussed *infra*.

[10] http://www.eeoc.gov/facts/pandemic_flu.html. For a more detailed discussion of this guidance see CRS Report R40866, *The Americans with Disabilities Act (ADA): Employment Issues and the 2009 Influenza Pandemic*, by Nancy Lee Jones.

[11] 42 U.S.C. §12113(b).

[12] 42 U.S.C. §12113(d). This provision was added in an amendment by Senator Hatch after a long debate over the Chapman Amendment which was not enacted. The Chapman Amendment would have allowed employers in businesses involved in food handling to exclude individuals with specific contagious diseases such as HIV infection. See 136 Cong. Rec. 10911 (1990).

[13] 42 U.S.C. §12182(3).

[14] 42 U.S.C. §12131(2).

[15] 480 U.S. 273, 287, note 16 (1987).

[16] S.Rept. 101-116, 101st Cong., 1st Sess. reprinted in Vol. I, Committee Print Serial No. 102-A *Legislative History of P.L. 101-336 The Americans with Disabilities Act,* prepared for the House Committee on Education and Labor at 139 (Dec. 1990).

[17] H.Rept. 101-485, 101st Cong., 2nd Sess., reprinted in Vol. I, Committee Print Serial No. 102-A *Legislative History of P.L. 101-336 The Americans with Disabilities Act,* prepared for the House Committee on Education and Labor at 349 (Dec. 1990). See also 136 Cong. Rec. 10858 (1990).

[18] 75 FED. REG.. 56163 (September 15, 2010). For a general discussion of these regulations see CRS Report R41376, *The Americans with Disabilities Act (ADA): Final Rule Amending Title II and Title III Regulations*, by Nancy Lee Jones.

[19] 28 C.F.R. §35.39(a) (2010)(title II); 28 C.F.R. §36.208(a) (2010)(title III).

[20] 28 C.F.R. §35.39(b) (2010)(title II); 28 C.F.R. §36.208(b) (2010)(title III).

[21] 480 U.S. 273, 287, footnote 16 (1987).

[22] *Id.* at 287.

[23] *Id.* at 288.

[24] *Id.*

[25] *Arline v. School Bd. of Nassau County,* 692 F.Supp. 1286 (M.D. Fla. 1988).

[26] 524 U.S. 624 (1998).

[27] *Abbott v. Bragdon,* 163 F.3d 87 (1st Cir. 1998), *cert. den.,* 526 U.S. 1131(1999).

[28] 536 U.S. 73 (2002).

[29] 42 U.S.C. §12113(a).

[30] 42 U.S.C. §12113(b).

[31] 226 F.3d 1063 (9th Cir. 2000).

[32] 29 C.F.R. §1630.15(b)(2).

[33] See e.g., *Montalvo v. Radcliffe,* 167 F.3d 873 (4th Cir. 1999), *cert. denied,* 528 U.S. 813 (1999), where the fourth circuit held that excluding a child who has HIV from karate classes did not violate the ADA because the child posed a significant risk to the health and safety of others which could not be eliminated by reasonable modification.

[34] See e.g., *Lassiter v. Reno*, 885 F.Supp. 869 (E.D.Va. 1995), *aff'd* 86 F.3d 1151 (4th Cir. 1996), *cert. denied,* 519 U.S. 1091 (1997), where the court found that a deputy U.S. Marshal diagnosed as suffering from delusional paranoid personality disorder presented a reasonable probability of substantial harm if permitted to carry a firearm.

[35] See e.g., *Doe v. Woodford County Board of Education,* 213 F.3d 921 (6th Cir. 2000), where the court upheld the school's decision to place a student who was a hemophiliac and a carrier of the hepatitis B virus on hold status for the varsity basketball team pending a medical clearance.

[36] For a discussion of several of these cases see Jeffrey A. Van Detta, "'Typhoid Mary' Meets the ADA: A Case Study of the 'Direct Threat' Standard under the Americans with Disabilities Act," 22 Harv. J. of Law and Public Policy 849, 868-923 (1999); and Brian S. Prestes, "Disciplining the Americans with Disabilities Act Direct Threat Defense," 22 Berkeley J. Emp. & Labor Law 409, 422-434 (2001).

In: The Americans with Disabilities Act (ADA): Provisions...   ISBN: 978-1-61470-961-9
Editor: John Kiviniemi and Cécile Sanjo   © 2012 Nova Science Publishers, Inc.

Chapter 9

THE AMERICANS WITH DISABILITIES ACT: APPLICATION TO THE INTERNET

Nancy Lee Jones

SUMMARY

The Americans with Disabilities Act (ADA) provides broad nondiscrimination protection in employment, public services, public accommodations, and services operated by private entities, transportation, and telecommunications for individuals with disabilities. As stated in the act, its purpose is "to provide a clear and comprehensive national mandate for the elimination of discrimination against individuals with disabilities."

However, the ADA, enacted on July 26, 1990, prior to widespread use of the Internet, does not specifically cover the Internet, and the issue of coverage has not been definitively resolved. The Supreme Court has not addressed this issue, although there are some lower court decisions. The cases that directly discuss the ADA's application to the Internet vary in their conclusions about coverage. On July 23, 2010, the Department of Justice issued an advanced notice of proposed rulemaking which would require Internet accessibility.

INTRODUCTION

The Americans with Disabilities Act (ADA)[1] has often been described as the most sweeping nondiscrimination legislation since the Civil Rights Act of 1964. It provides broad nondiscrimination protection in employment, public services, public accommodations, and services operated by private entities, transportation, and telecommunications[2] for individuals with disabilities. As stated in the act, its purpose is "to provide a clear and comprehensive national mandate for the elimination of discrimination against individuals with disabilities."

However, the ADA, enacted on July 26, 1990, prior to widespread use of the Internet, does not specifically cover the Internet, and the issue of coverage has not been definitively resolved.[3] The Supreme Court has not addressed this issue, although there are some lower court decisions. Similarly, congressional action has been limited. The ADA was amended in

2008 to respond to a series of Supreme Court decisions that had interpreted the definition of disability narrowly but did not address the issue of Internet coverage.[4] On April 22, 2010, the Subcommittee on the Constitution, Civil Rights, and Civil Liberties of the House Judiciary Committee held a hearing on the ADA in the digital age.[5] On July 23, 2010, the Department of Justice issued an advanced notice of proposed rulemaking which would require Internet accessibility.[6]

On October 8, 2010, President Obama signed the Equal Access to 21st Century Communications Act, P.L. 111-260. Although this law does not amend the ADA, it requires, in part, certain access to Internet-based services and equipment for individuals with disabilities.

The American Recovery and Reinvestment Act (ARRA)[7] did not specifically mention Internet accessibility, but did include the Health Information Technology for Economic and Clinical Health (HITECH) Act as part of P.L. 111-5,[8] and also directed the Federal Communications Commission (FCC) to develop a national broadband plan. The FCC released its plan on March 16, 2010.[9] One of the recommendations in this plan stated:

> The federal government should ensure the accessibility of digital content. The DOJ should amend its regulations to clarify the obligations of commercial establishments under Title III of the Americans with Disabilities Act with respect to commercial websites. The FCC should open a proceeding on the accessibility of video programming distributed over the Internet, the devices used to display such programming and related user interfaces, video programming guides and menus. Congress should consider clarifying the FCC's authority to adopt video description rules.[10]

The ADA contains various requirements depending on whether the discrimination prohibited is in the employment context (Title I), is related to the activities of state or local governments (Title II), or concerns public accommodations (Title III). Although most of the judicial decisions and discussion of ADA applicability to the Internet have arisen regarding public accommodations, it is helpful to briefly examine employment and state and local government requirements.

EMPLOYMENT

Statutory Language

Title I of the ADA, as amended by the ADA Amendments Act of 2008, provides that no covered entity shall discriminate against a qualified individual on the basis of disability in regard to job application procedures; the hiring, advancement, or discharge of employees; employee compensation; job training; or other terms, conditions, and privileges of employment.[11] The term employer is defined as a person engaged in an industry affecting commerce who has 15 or more employees.[12] If the issue raised under the ADA is employment related, and the threshold issues of meeting the definition of an individual with a disability and involving an employer employing more than 15 individuals are met, the next step is to determine whether the individual is a qualified individual with a disability who, with or without reasonable accommodation, can perform the essential functions of the job.

Title I defines a "qualified individual with a disability." Such an individual is "an individual with a disability who, with or without reasonable accommodation, can perform the essential functions of the employment position that such person holds or desires."[13] The ADA requires the provision of reasonable accommodation unless the accommodation would pose an undue hardship on the operation of the business.[14]

"Reasonable accommodation" is defined in the ADA as including making existing facilities readily accessible to and usable by individuals with disabilities, job restructuring, part-time or modified work schedules, reassignment to a vacant position, acquisition or modification of equipment or devices, adjustment of examinations or training materials or policies, provision of qualified readers or interpreters, or other similar accommodations.[15] "Undue hardship" is defined as "an action requiring significant difficulty or expense."[16] Factors to be considered in determining whether an action would create an undue hardship include the nature and cost of the accommodation, the overall financial resources of the facility, the overall financial resources of the covered entity, and the type of operation or operations of the covered entity.

Judicial and Regulatory Interpretations

The ADA's statutory language specifically prohibits discrimination in "other terms, conditions, and privileges of employment."[17] The National Council on Disability (NCD)[18] has observed that "[n]o case or serious scholarly or legal argument has ever been found to support the proposition that because a job's functions involve electronic communication, employers are relieved of the obligation to consider reasonable accommodations or other measures aimed at facilitating equal access to the tools of the trade."[19] However, no judicial cases were found that specifically mandated website accessibility in the employment context. Despite this dearth of case law, it could be argued that Equal Employment Opportunity Commission (EEOC) policies on telework,[20] which is generally performed using computers, indicate that employment discrimination can encompass the lack of access to the Internet.[21]

STATE AND LOCAL GOVERNMENTS

Statutory Language

Title II of the ADA provides that no qualified individual with a disability shall be excluded from participation in or be denied the benefits of the services, programs, or activities of a public entity or be subjected to discrimination by any such entity.[22] "Public entity" is defined as state and local governments, any department or other instrumentality of a state or local government and certain transportation authorities. The ADA does not apply to the executive branch of the federal government; the executive branch and the U.S. Postal Service are covered by Section 504 of the Rehabilitation Act of 1973.[23]

The Department of Justice (DOJ) regulations for Title II contain a specific section on program accessibility. Each service, program, or activity conducted by a public entity, when viewed in its entirety, must be readily accessible to and usable by individuals with disabilities. However, a public entity is not required to make each of its existing facilities accessible.[24] Program accessibility is limited in certain situations involving historic preservation. In addition, in meeting the program accessibility requirement, a public entity is not required to take any action that would result in a fundamental alteration in the nature of its service, program, or activity or in undue financial and administrative burdens.[25]

Judicial Interpretations

Like Title I, the case law and regulatory interpretations regarding the application of the ADA to the Internet are sparse under Title II.[26] However, one district court has examined accessibility issues regarding the website of a public transit system. In *Martin v. Metropolitan Atlanta Rapid Transit Authority*,[27] the court addressed a number of accessibility issues involving the Atlanta transit authority, including information accessibility. Noting that the information was available in several forms, including a website, the court found that the information was not equally accessible to individuals with disabilities even though some information was available by telephone. The court stated the following:

> MARTA representatives also concede that the system's web page is not formatted in such a way that it can be read by persons who are blind but who are capable of using text reader computer software for the visually impaired.... However, it now appears that MARTA is attempting to correct this problem. Until these deficiencies are corrected, MARTA is violating the ADA mandate of "making adequate communications capacity available, through accessible formats and technology, to enable users to obtain information and schedule service."[28]

Department of Justice and Department of Education Interpretations Regarding the Internet

On July 23, 2010, the Department of Justice issued an advanced notice of proposed rulemaking which would require Internet accessibility.[29] In the April 2010 hearings before the House Judiciary Committee, Samuel R. Bagenstos, Principal Deputy Assistant Attorney General for Civil Rights at the Department of Justice, testified that "[t]here is no doubt that the Internet sites of State and local government entities are covered by Title II of the ADA."[30] He also noted that DOJ has published technical assistance, "Accessibility of State and Local Government Websites to People with Disabilities,"[31] which provides guidance for making government websites accessible.[32]

The concept of effective communications was also at issue in investigations by the Office of Civil Rights (OCR) at the Department of Education (ED). These OCR investigations involved access to various class and course related materials, including campus computer labs and the Internet, and generally resulted in required access.[33]

PUBLIC ACCOMMODATIONS

Statutory Provisions

Title III provides that no individual shall be discriminated against on the basis of disability in the full and equal enjoyment of the goods, services, facilities, privileges, advantages, or accommodations of any place of public accommodation by any person who owns, leases (or leases to), or operates a place of public accommodation.[34] Entities that are covered by the term "public accommodation" are listed, and include, among others, hotels, restaurants, theaters, auditoriums, laundromats, travel services, museums, parks, zoos, private schools, day care centers, professional offices of health care providers, and gymnasiums.[35] Religious institutions or entities controlled by religious institutions are not included on the list.

There are some limitations on the nondiscrimination requirements, and a failure to remove architectural barriers is not a violation unless such a removal is "readily achievable."[36] "Readily achievable" is defined as meaning "easily accomplishable and able to be carried out without much difficulty or expense."[37] Reasonable modifications in practices, policies, or procedures are required unless they would fundamentally alter the nature of the goods, services, facilities, or privileges or they would result in an undue burden.[38] An undue burden is defined as an action involving "significant difficulty or expense."[39]

Department of Justice Interpretations

The Department of Justice on July 23, 2010 issued an advanced notice of proposed rulemaking which would require Internet accessibility.[40] Samuel R. Bagenstos, Principal Deputy Assistant Attorney General for Civil Rights at the Department of Justice, testified in the April 2010 hearings before the House Judiciary Committee that although case law has been limited, "the position of the Department of Justice has been clear: Title III applies to the Internet sites and services of private entities that meet the definition of public accommodations set forth in the statute and implementing regulations."[41] He also noted that DOJ is considering issuing guidance regarding the Internet sites of private businesses that are considered public accommodations under Title III of the ADA.[42] Mr. Bagenstos observed that the Department's position was first articulated in a response to a congressional inquiry. This response stated that "[c]overed entities that use the Internet for communications regarding their programs, goods, or services must be prepared to offer those communications through accessible means as well."[43]

DOJ has also argued that the ADA covers the Internet in amicus briefs.[44] In its report on the activities of the House Judiciary Committee following the hearings on the ADA and Internet accessibility on February 9, 2000, the House Judiciary Committee stated that "[i]t is the opinion of the Department of Justice that the ADA's accessibility requirements do apply to private Internet web sites and services."[45]

Place of Public Accommodation

As discussed previously, Title III prohibits discrimination in the full and equal enjoyment of the goods, services, facilities, privileges, advantages, or accommodations of any *place* of public accommodation by any person who owns, leases (or leases to), or operates a *place* of public accommodation.[46] One of the relevant issues in resolving the matter of whether Title III of the ADA applies to the Internet is whether a place of public accommodation is limited to actual physical structures.

Public Accommodations are not Limited to Physical Structures

The courts have split on this issue with the First Circuit in *Carparts Distribution Center v. Automotive Wholesalers Association of New England Inc.,*[47] finding that public accommodations are not limited to actual physical structures. The court reasoned that

> [b]y including "travel service" among the list of services considered "public accommodations," Congress clearly contemplated that "service establishments" include providers of services which do not require a person to physically enter an actual physical structure. Many travel services conduct business by telephone or correspondence without requiring their customers to enter an office in order to obtain their services. Likewise, one can easily imagine the existence of other service establishments conducting business by mail and phone without providing facilities for their customers to enter in order to utilize their services. It would be irrational to conclude that persons who enter an office to purchase services are protected by the ADA, but persons who purchase the same services over the telephone or by mail are not. Congress could not have intended such an absurd result.[48]

The First Circuit concluded that "to exclude this broad category of businesses from the reach of Title III and limit the application of Title III to physical structures which persons must enter to obtain goods and services would run afoul of the purposes of the ADA."[49]

The Seventh Circuit in *Doe v. Mutual of Omaha Insurance Company*[50] agreed with the First Circuit. In *Doe,* Judge Posner discussed the nondiscrimination requirements of Title III in the context of a case involving a cap on insurance policies for AIDS and AIDS-related complications and found that "[t]he core meaning of this provision, plainly enough, is that the owner or operator of a store, hotel, restaurant, dentist's office, travel agency, theater, website, or other facility (whether in physical space or in electronic space) ... that is open to the public cannot exclude disabled persons from entering the facility and, once in, from using the facility in the same way that the nondisabled do."[51] The court reasoned that "the owner or operator of, say, a camera store can neither bar the door to the disabled nor let them in but then refuse to sell its cameras to them on the same terms as to other customers."[52] However, Judge Posner found no violation of the ADA in this case and concluded that "Section 302(a) does not require a seller to alter his product to make it equally valuable to the disabled and nondisabled."[53]

The Second Circuit joined the First and Seventh Circuits in finding that the ADA is not limited to physical access. The court in *Pallozzi v. Allstate Life Insurance Co.,*[54] stated that "Title III's mandate that the disabled be accorded 'full and equal enjoyment of goods, [and] services ... of any place of public accommodation,' suggests to us that the statute was meant to guarantee them more than mere physical access."

Public Accommodations are Limited to Physical Structures

In contrast to the cases discussed above, the Third, Sixth, Ninth, and Eleventh Circuits apparently restrict the concept of public accommodations to physical places.

In *Stoutenborough v. National Football League, Inc.,*[55] the Sixth Circuit dealt with a case brought by an association of individuals with hearing impairments who filed suit against the National Football League (NFL) and several television stations under Title III alleging that the NFL's blackout rule discriminated against them since they had no other way of accessing football games when live telecasts are prohibited. The Sixth Circuit rejected this allegation holding that the prohibitions of Title III are restricted to places of public accommodations. Similarly, in *Parker v. Metropolitan Life Insurance Co.,*[56] the Sixth Circuit held that the ADA's nondiscrimination prohibition relating to public accommodations did not prohibit an employer from providing employees a disability plan that provided longer benefits for employees disabled by physical illness than those disabled by mental illness. In arriving at this holding, the Sixth Circuit found that "a benefit plan offered by an employer is not a good offered by a place of public accommodation.... A public accommodation is a physical place."[57]

In *Ford v. Schering-Plough Corp.*[58] and *Weyer v. Twentieth Century Fox Film Corp.,*[59] the Third and Ninth Circuits also found that a public accommodation must be a physical place. As the Third Circuit in *Ford* stated,

> [t]he plain meaning of Title III is that a public accommodation is a place.... This is in keeping with the host of examples of public accommodations provided by the ADA, all of which refer to places.... Since Ford received her disability benefits via her employment at Schering, she had no nexus to MetLife's 'insurance office' and thus was not discriminated against in connection with a public accommodation.[60]

The Eleventh Circuit used similar reasoning in *Access Now, Inc. v. Southwest Airlines*, a case directly involved the ADA and the Internet. [61]

Judicial Decisions on Title III and the Internet

As noted above, the precise issue of the ADA's application to the Internet arose in *Access Now, Inc., v. Southwest Airlines, Co.*, where the district court held that the Southwest Airlines website was not a "place of public accommodation" and therefore was not covered by the ADA. The district court examined the ADA's statutory language, noting that all of the listed categories were concrete places, and that to expand the ADA to cover "virtual" spaces would be to create new rights.

Previously, on November 2, 1999, the National Federation of the Blind (NFB) filed a complaint against America Online (AOL) in federal district court alleging that AOL violated Title III of the ADA. NFB and other blind plaintiffs stated that they could only independently use computers by concurrently running screen access software programs for the blind that convert visual information into synthesized speech or braille. They alleged that AOL had designed its service so that it is incompatible with screen access software programs for the blind, failing "to remove communications barriers presented by its designs thus denying the blind independent access to this service, in violation of Title III of the ADA, 42 U.S.C. §12181, et seq."[62] The case was settled on July 26, 2000.[63]

The most recent judicial decision on the ADA application to the Internet is *National Federation of the Blind v. Target Corporation.*[64] In *National Federation of the Blind,* the district court, taking a more nuanced approach, denied Target's motion to dismiss to the extent it alleged that the inaccessibility of the retailer's web site impeded the full and equal enjoyment of goods and services offered in the retailer's stores. The motion to dismiss was granted in part concerning the aspects of the website that offered information and services unconnected to the retailer's store. The court noted that the purpose of the ADA was "broader than mere physical access" and that "[t]o the extent defendant argues that plaintiffs' claims are not cognizable because they occur away from a 'place' of public accommodation, defendant's argument must fail." The court required that there be a "nexus" between the Internet services and the physical place in order to present an actionable ADA claim.

The use of the "nexus" approach to the ADA's applicability to the Internet would cover many places of business such as Target. However, stores such as Amazon.com that have no physical storefront may not be covered under such an approach. The nexus approach has been criticized by the National Council of Disability:

> With the passage of time, as more and more goods, services, informational resources, recreation, communication, social and interactive activities of all kind migrate, wholly or partly, to the Net, maintenance of legal distinctions among otherwise similar Web sites, based on their connection or lack of connection to a physical facility, will become increasingly untenable and incoherent. Were there no nexus doctrine, and were all Web sites to be per se excluded from coverage, the law, however unjust, would at least be clear. But now that we see the direction in which the law, even in the hands of its most cautious interlocutors, is moving, the effort to define what is a sufficient nexus and to determine whether it exists in each particular case will surely continue. Use of the nexus approach, preferable as it may be to civil rights advocates over an approach that categorically excludes the Web from coverage, may, however, result in far more havoc than even the most sweeping and inclusive requirement for across-the-board commercial Web site accessibility ever could.[65]

CONCLUSION

The ADA was enacted in 1990, prior to widespread use of the Internet and does not specifically cover the Internet. Similarly, the ADA regulations do not specifically mention the Internet. However, the Department of Justice, on July 23, 2010, issued an advanced notice of proposed rulemaking which would require Internet accessibility. There has been no Supreme Court decision on point, and there have been few lower court judicial decisions. The lower courts that have examined the issue have split, creating some uncertainty. In addition, the use of a "nexus" approach in *National Federation of the Blind v. Target Corporation,* requiring a connection between the Internet services and the physical place in order to present an actionable ADA claim, would limit the application of the ADA to online retailers. Despite this uncertainty, it would appear likely that the Department of Justice's position would prevail, especially in light of the ADA's broad nondiscrimination mandate.

End Notes

[1] 42 U.S.C. §12101 *et seq.* For a more detailed discussion of the ADA see CRS Report 98-921, *The Americans with Disabilities Act (ADA): Statutory Language and Recent Issues*, by Nancy Lee Jones.

[2] Title IV of the ADA amends Title II of the Communications Act of 1934 to ensure that individuals with hearing impairments are able to use telephones. 47 U.S.C. §225. One commentator has argued that Congress should use Title IV of the ADA as a model for adding an amendment specifically applying the ADA to the Internet. See Katherine Rengel, "The Americans with Disabilities Act and Internet Accessibility for the Blind," 25 John Marshall HJ. Computer & Info. L. 543 (2008).

[3] For a discussion of this issue see National Council on Disability (NCD), "The Need for Federal Legislation and Regulation Prohibiting Telecommunications and Information Services Discrimination," http://www.ncd.gov/ newsroom/publications/2006/pdf/discrimination.pdf. See also National Council on Disability (NCD), "National Disability Policy: A Progress Report" March 31, 2009, http://www.ncd.gov/newsroom/publications/2009/pdf/ ProgressReport.pdf. It should be noted that federal government websites are required to be accessible under a separate statute, Section 508 of the Rehabilitation Act, 29 U.S.C. §794(d), as amended by P.L. 105-220. Section 508 requires that the electronic and information technology used by federal agencies be accessible to individuals with disabilities, including employees and members of the public. Generally, Section 508 requires each federal department or agency and the U.S. Postal Service to ensure that individuals with disabilities who are federal employees have access to and use of electronic and information technology that is comparable to that of individuals who do not have disabilities. For more detailed information see http://www.section508.gov.

[4] The ADA Amendments Act, P.L. 110-325. For a more detailed discussion of P.L. 110-325, see CRS Report RL34691, *The ADA Amendments Act: P.L. 110-325*, by Nancy Lee Jones.

[5] Achieving the Promise of the Americans with Disabilities Act in the Digital Age – Current Issues, Challenges, and Opportunities: Hearing Before the H. Subcommittee on the Constitution, Civil Rights, and Civil Liberties of the H. Comm. on the Judiciary, 110th Cong., 2d Sess. (2010), http://judiciary.house.gov/hearings/hear_100422_1.html. Ten years earlier, hearings had also been held on the applicability of the ADA to private Internet sites, Applicability of the Americans with Disabilities Act (ADA) to Private Internet Sites: Hearing Before the H. Subcommittee on the Constitution of the H. Comm. on the Judiciary, 106th Cong. (2000).

[6] http://www.ada.gov/anprm2010/web%20anprm_2010.htm.

[7] P.L. 111-5.

[8] The HITECH Act is intended to promote the widespread adoption of health information technology (HIT) to support the electronic sharing of clinical data among hospitals, physicians, and other health care stakeholders. For a discussion of HITECH see CRS Report R40161, *The Health Information Technology for Economic and Clinical Health (HITECH) Act*, by C. Stephen Redhead.

[9] FCC, "Connecting America: The National Broadband Plan," http://www.broadband.gov/download-plan/.

[10] *Id.* at p. 182.

[11] 42 U.S.C. §12112(a), as amended by P.L. 110-325, §5. The ADA Amendments Act strikes the prohibition of discrimination against a qualified individual with a disability because of the disability of such individual and substitutes the prohibition of discrimination against a qualified individual "on the basis of disability." The Senate Managers' Statement noted that this change "ensures that the emphasis in questions of disability discrimination is properly on the critical inquiry of whether a qualified person has been discriminated against on the basis of disability, and not unduly focused on the preliminary question of whether a particular person is a 'person with a disability.'" 153 CONG. REC. S8347 (Sept. 11, 2008)(Statement of Managers to Accompany S. 3406, the Americans with Disabilities Act Amendments Act of 2008).

[12] 42 U.S.C. §12111(5).

[13] 42 U.S.C. §1211(8). The EEOC has stated that a function may be essential because (1) the position exists to perform the duty, (2) there are a limited number of employees available who could perform the function, or (3) the function is highly specialized. 29 C.F.R. §1630(n)(2).

[14] See 45 C.F.R. Part 84.

[15] 42 U.S.C. § 12111(9).

[16] 42 U.S.C. §12111(10).

[17] 42 U.S.C. §12112(a), as amended by P.L. 110-325, §5.

[18] NCD is an independent federal agency that provides advice to the President, Congress, and executive branch agencies to promote policies, programs, practices, and procedures that guarantee equal opportunity for all individuals with disabilities. See http://www.ncd.gov.

[19] National Council on Disability, "When the Americans with Disabilities Act Goes Online: Application of the ADA to the Internet and the Worldwide Web," (July 10, 2003) http://www.ncd.gov/newsroom/ publications/2003/ adainternet.htm.

[20] EEOC, Fact Sheet: Work at Home: Telework as a Reasonable Accommodation (February 3, 2003), http://www.eeoc.gov/facts/telework.html.

[21] In addition, the National Federation of the Blind of Arkansas, the state of Arkansas, and the software provider SAP Public Services, Inc., entered into a settlement agreement in 2008 to resolve a suit by blind state employees who could not access the Arkansas administrative statewide information system. See http://www.NFB.org.

[22] 42 U.S.C. §§12131-12133.

[23] 29 U.S.C. §794.

[24] 28 C.F.R. §35.150.

[25] *Id.*

[26] For a discussion of how Titles II and III of the ADA might apply to internet access by students see Judith Stilz Ogden and Lawrence Menter, "Inaccessible School Webpages: Are Remedies Available?" 38 J. L. & Educ. 393 (2009).

[27] 225 F.Supp.2d 1362 (N.D. Ga. 2002).

[28] *Id.* at 1377. Quoting from the Department of Transportation ADA regulations, 49 C.F.R. §37.167(f).

[29] http://www.ada.gov/anprm2010/web%20anprm_2010.htm.

[30] *Achieving the Promise of the Americans with Disabilities Act in the Digital Age – Current Issues, Challenges, and Opportunities: Hearing Before the H. Subcommittee on the Constitution, Civil Rights, and Civil Liberties of the H. Comm. on the Judiciary,* 110th Cong., 2d Sess. (2010), http://judiciary.house.gov/hearings/hear_100422_1.html; testimony of Samuel R. Bagenstos, Principal Deputy Assistant Attorney General for Civil Rights at the Department of Justice, http://judiciary.house.gov/hearings/pdf/Bagenstos100422.pdf.

[31] See http://www.usdoj.gov/crt/ada/websites2.htm.

[32] *Achieving the Promise of the Americans with Disabilities Act in the Digital Age – Current Issues, Challenges, and Opportunities: Hearing Before the H. Subcommittee on the Constitution, Civil Rights, and Civil Liberties of the H. Comm. on the Judiciary,* 110th Cong., 2d Sess. (2010), http://judiciary.house.gov/hearings/hear_100422_1.html; testimony of Samuel R. Bagenstos, Principal Deputy Assistant Attorney General for Civil Rights at the Department of Justice, http://judiciary.house.gov/hearings/pdf/Bagenstos100422.pdf.

[33] See http://people.rit.edu/easi/law.htm. For a more detailed discussion of this issue see National Council on Disability, "When the Americans with Disabilities Act Goes Online: Application of the ADA to the Internet and the Worldwide Web," (July 10, 2003) http://www.ncd.gov/newsroom/publications/2003/adainternet.htm.

[34] 42 U.S.C. §12182.

[35] 42 U.S.C. §12181.

[36] 42 U.S.C. §12182(b)(2)(A)(iv).

[37] 42 U.S.C. §12181.

[38] 42 U.S.C. §12182(b)(2)(A).

[39] 28 C.F.R. §36.104.

[40] http://www.ada.gov/anprm2010/web%20anprm_2010.htm.

[41] Achieving the Promise of the Americans with Disabilities Act in the Digital Age – Current Issues, Challenges, and Opportunities: Hearing Before the H. Subcommittee on the Constitution, Civil Rights, and Civil Liberties of the H. Comm. on the Judiciary, 110th Cong., 2d Sess. (2010), http://judiciary.house.gov/hearings/hear_100422_1.html; testimony of Samuel R. Bagenstos, Principal Deputy Assistant Attorney General for Civil Rights at the Department of Justice, http://judiciary.house.gov/hearings/pdf/Bagenstos100422.pdf. In his testimony, Mr. Bagenstos also observed that accessibility issues arise in other technologies as well, and he specifically noted the increased use of electronic book readers by schools. DOJ and the Department of Education sent a joint letter to college and university presidents expressing concern about the use of inaccessible readers. See http://www.ada.gov/kindle_ltr_eddoj.htm. In addition, DOJ has resolved complaints against several universities concerning the use of inaccessible readers. See e.g., http://www.ada.gov/case_western_univ.htm; http://www.ada.gov/reed_college.htm; http://www.ada.gov/pace_univ.htm; http://www.ada.gov/princeton.htm.

[42] *Id.*

[43] Letter from Deval L. Patrick, Assistant Attorney General, Civil Rights Division, to Tom Harkin, U.S. Senator (September 9, 1996) http://www.usdoj.gov/crt/foia/tal712.txt One commentator has argued that this letter is limited in its scope since it applies its requirements only to "covered entities" which the letter defined as state and local governments and places of public accommodation. See Katherine Rengel, "The Americans with Disabilities Act and Internet Accessibility for the Blind," 25 John Marshal J. of Computer & Information Law 543 (2008).

[44] See e.g., Amicus Brief of the United States filed in the Fifth Circuit in Hooks v. OKBridge, Inc. (No 99-50891) "The language of the statute is broad enough to cover services provided over this new medium and courts are not reluctant to apply old words to new technology in a way that is consistent with modern usage and legislative intent." http://www.usdoj.gov/crt/briefs/hooks.htm.

[45] H.Rept. 106-1048, at 275 (2001). One commentator has argued that this statement, combined with the lack of congressional action, indicates that Congress is "deferring to the DOJ's authority to promulgate rules implementing Title III instead of amending Title III or drafting new legislation." Ali Abrar and Kerry J. Dingle, "From Madness to Method: the Americans with Disabilities Act Meets the Internet" 44 Harv. C.R.-C.L. L. Rev. 133, 155 (2009).

[46] 42 U.S.C. §12182 (emphasis added).

[47] *Carparts Distribution Center, Inc. v. Automotive Wholesalers' Association of New England, Inc.,* 37 F.3d 12 (1st Cir. 1994).

[48] *Id.* at 22.

[49] *Id.* at 26-27.

[50] 179 F.3d 557 (7th Cir. 1999), *cert. denied,* 528 U.S. 1106 (2000).

[51] *Id.* at 559 (emphasis added.)

[52] *Id.*

[53] *Id.* at 563.

[54] 198 F.3d 28 (2d Cir. 1999).

[55] 59 F.3d 580 (6th Cir. 1995), *cert. denied,* 516 U.S. 1028 (1995).

[56] 121 F.3d 1006 (6th Cir. 1997), *cert. denied,* 522 U.S. 1084 (1998).

[57] *Id.* At 1010. See also, *Lenox v. Healthwise of Kentucky,* 149 F.3d 453 (6th Cir. 1999).

[58] 145 F.3d 601 (3rd Cir. 1998).

[59] 198 F.3d 1104 (9th Cir. 2000).

[60] 145 F.3d 601, 613 (3rd Cir. 1998).

[61] 227 F.Supp.2d 1312 (S.D. Fla. 2002), appeal dismissed on other grounds, 385 F.3d 1324 (11th Cir. 2004). But see Rendon v. Valleycrest Productions, 294 F.3rd 1279 (11th Cir. 2002), where the Eleventh Circuit found a violation of the ADA in the use of telephone selection process that tended to screen out individuals with disabilities.

[62] *National Federation of the Blind v. America Online,* Complaint, http://www.nfb.org/Images/nfb/Publications/bm/bm99/brlm9912.htm (November 2, 1999).

[63] The settlement agreement can be found at the National Federation of the Blind website, http://www.nfb.org.

[64] 452 F.Supp.2d 946 (N.D. Calif. 2006). The case was settled on August 27, 2008. See http://www.nfb.org. For a more detailed discussion of this case see Isabel Arana DuPree, "Websites as 'Places of Public Accommodation': Amending the Americans with Disabilities Act in the Wake of *National Federal of the Blind v. Target Corporation,*" NC J. L. & Tech. 273 (2007); Jeffrey Bashaw, "Applying the Americans with Disabilities Act to Private Websites after *National Federation of the Blind v. Target,*" 4 Shidler J. L. Com. & Tech. 3 (2008).

[65] National Council on Disability, "When the Americans with Disabilities Act Goes Online: Application of the ADA to the Internet and the Worldwide Web," (July 10, 2003) http://www.ncd.gov/newsroom/publications/2003/ adainternet.htm. See also Nikki D. Kessling, "Why the Target 'Nexus Test' Leaves Disabled Americans Disconnected: A Better Approach to Determine Whether Private Commercial Websites are 'Places of Public Accommodations,'" 45 Houston L. Rev. 991 (2008) where the author argued that the nexus test does not reflect statutory intent and that ADA coverage of a website should depend on the website's "commerciality and character;" Ali Abrar and Kerry J. Dingle, "From Madness to Method: The Americans with Disabilities Act Meets the Internet," 44 Harv. C.R.-C.L. L. Rev. 133 (2009), where is it argued that the nexus test is both under and over inclusive.

In: The Americans with Disabilities Act (ADA): Provisions... ISBN: 978-1-61470-961-9
Editor: John Kiviniemi and Cécile Sanjo © 2012 Nova Science Publishers, Inc.

Chapter 10

THE AMERICANS WITH DISABILITIES ACT (ADA): MOVIE CAPTIONING AND VIDEO DESCRIPTION

Nancy Lee Jones

SUMMARY

The Americans with Disabilities Act (ADA) is a broad civil rights statute prohibiting discrimination against individuals with disabilities. Title III of the ADA prohibits discrimination by public accommodations, which are defined to include movie theaters, but the statute does not include specific language on closed captioning or video description. Although the Department of Justice (DOJ) has promulgated regulations under Title III, it has not specifically addressed issues regarding closed captioning or video description. However, DOJ has issued an advance notice of proposed rulemaking (ANPR) to establish requirements for closed captioning and video description for movie theaters. The ANPR asks for input in several areas including the implications of a sliding compliance schedule, and the appropriate basis for calculating the number of movies that will be captioned and video described. In addition, the Ninth Circuit, in the first court of appeals case to address the issue, held that the ADA requires the provision of closed captioning and descriptive narration in movie theaters unless to do so would be a fundamental alteration or an undue burden.

INTRODUCTION

The Americans with Disabilities Act (ADA) is a broad civil rights statute prohibiting discrimination against individuals with disabilities.[1] As stated in the act, its purpose is "to provide a clear and comprehensive national mandate for the elimination of discrimination against individuals with disabilities."[2] Title III of the ADA prohibits discrimination by public accommodations, which are defined to include movie theaters, but the statute does not include specific language on closed captioning or video description.[3] The Department of Justice (DOJ) has promulgated regulations under Title III,[4] but has not specifically addressed issues regarding closed captioning[5] or video description.[6] However, DOJ has issued an advance notice of proposed rulemaking (ANPR) to establish requirements for closed captioning and video description for movie theaters.[7] In addition, the Ninth Circuit, in the first court of appeals case to address the issue, held that the ADA requires the provision of closed captioning and descriptive narration in movie theaters unless to do so would be a fundamental alteration or an undue burden.[8]

STATUTORY LANGUAGE AND LEGISLATIVE HISTORY

Title III of the ADA prohibits discrimination in "the full and equal enjoyment of the goods, services, facilities, privileges, advantages, or accommodations of a place of public accommodation by any person who owns, leases (or leases to), or operates a place of public accommodation."[9] Public accommodations are defined as including "a motion picture house, theater, concert hall, stadium, or other place of exhibition entertainment."[10] Places of public accommodation are prohibited from providing individuals with disabilities a service that is not equal to that afforded individuals without disabilities.[11] In addition, public accommodations are required to take action to ensure that an individual with a disability is not excluded, denied services, or otherwise treated differently because of the absence of auxiliary aids and services "unless the entity can demonstrate that taking such steps would fundamentally alter the nature of the good, service, facility, privilege, advantage, or accommodation being offered or would result in an undue burden."[12] Auxiliary aids and services are defined as including "qualified interpreters or other effective methods of making aurally delivered materials available to individuals with hearing impairments; [and] qualified readers, taped tests, or other effective methods of making visually delivered materials available to individuals with visual impairments."[13] Although the ADA does not define "undue burden," the DOJ regulations define undue burden as meaning "significant difficulty or expense" and provide various factors to be considered in making this determination.[14]

When the ADA was enacted in 1990, the technology for closed captioning was limited. The legislative history of the ADA did not specifically discuss closed captions, but did discuss open captioning. Open captioning was not seen as required by the ADA but open captioned versions of films were encouraged and theaters were encouraged to have some preannounced screenings of open captioned films.[15] The House Education and Labor report also emphasized that advances in technology may change what the ADA requires:

> The Committee wishes to make it clear that technological advances can be expected to further enhance options for making meaningful and effective opportunities available to individuals with disabilities. Such advances may require public accommodations to provide auxiliary aids and services in the future which today would not be required because they would be held to impose undue burdens on such entities.[16]

DOJ ADVANCE NOTICE OF PROPOSED RULEMAKING

On July 26, 2010, the 20th anniversary of the enactment of the ADA, DOJ issued an advance notice of proposed rulemaking regarding movie captioning and video description.

DOJ examined the ADA's statutory language and found that "given the present state of technology, we believe that requirements of captioning and video description fit comfortably within the statutory text."[17] Although DOJ had raised some questions regarding closed captioning and video description in its 2008 notice of proposed rulemaking, no regulations on the subject were proposed, and none were included in the final rule.[18] In the ANPR, DOJ sought further public comment on several new issues and technical questions as well as the implications of the conversion to digital cinema for potential regulations.[19] The issues DOJ sought public comment on included the following:

- the implications of a sliding compliance schedule;
- the appropriate basis for calculating the number of movies that will be captioned and video described;
- whether movie theater owners and operators should be given the option to use open captioning;
- the number of movie theater owners or operators who have converted to digital cinema;
- whether there are specific protocols or standards for captioning and video description for digital cinema;
- whether DOJ should require a system of notifying individuals with disabilities in advance as to which movies provide captioning and video description;
- whether DOJ should consider a training requirement for movie theater personnel; and
- whether a proposed rule should be considered an economically significant regulatory act and, if so, are there alternative regulatory approaches to minimize such impact.[20]

ARIZONA V. HARKINS AMUSEMENT ENTERPRISES

The Ninth Circuit in *Arizona v. Harkins Amusement Enterprises*[21] became the first court of appeals to address the ADA's requirements concerning closed captioning and video descriptions. The court held that closed captioning and video descriptions may be required by the ADA but are subject to the ADA's fundamental alteration and undue burden exceptions.

Harkins involved a suit by two patrons of a theater, one with a hearing impairment and one with impaired vision. They alleged that the theater owners discriminated against them by not providing open or closed captioning and descriptive narration. The court examined the statutory language of the ADA, emphasizing the requirement for auxiliary aids and services and finding that "movie captioning and audio descriptions clearly are auxiliary aids and services."[22] Rejecting the defendant's argument that captioning and descriptive narration fall outside the scope of the ADA , the Ninth Circuit noted that the ADA makes it discriminatory to fail to take steps to ensure that an individual with a disability is not excluded "because of the absence of auxiliary aids and services."[23] The defendant also argued that DOJ's regulatory commentary specifically did not require open captioning, and the court agreed that the defendant should be able to rely on the plain meaning of DOJ's commentary until it was revised. However, the commentary did not address closed captioning, and the court returned to the statutory language regarding auxiliary aids for its analysis, finding that closed captioning and descriptive narration "fall comfortably within the scope of this definition."[24]

In addition, the court noted that several defenses were available to the defendant, including the arguments that closed captioning and descriptive narration would fundamentally alter the nature of its services or constitute an undue burden. Although the Ninth Circuit's decision is only binding in that circuit, its decision provided an added impetus to DOJ's consideration of regulations in the area.[25]

End Notes

[1] For a more detailed discussion of the ADA see CRS Report 98-921, *The Americans with Disabilities Act (ADA): Statutory Language and Recent Issues*, by Nancy Lee Jones.

[2] 42 U.S.C. §12101(b)(1).

[3] 42 U.S.C. §12181(7)(C).

[4] 28 C.F.R. Part 36. For a discussion of recent changes to these regulations see CRS Report R41376, *The Americans with Disabilities Act (ADA): Final Rule Amending Title II and Title III Regulations*, by Nancy Lee Jones.

[5] Closed captioning is a process that displays the written text of a movie's dialog and other sounds only to those who request it by means such as a personal digital assistant (PDA). 75 FED. REG. 43470 (July 26, 2010).

[6] Video description allows individuals with visual impairments to access movies by providing a spoken narration of key visual elements. 75 FED. REG. 43470 (July 26, 2010).

[7] 75 FED. REG. 43467 (July 26, 2010). On the same date, DOJ also issued ANPRs on Accessibility of Web Information and Services Provided by Entities Covered by the ADA, Accessibility of Next Generation 9-1-1, and Accessibility of Equipment and Furniture. These other ANPRs are beyond the scope of this report. For a discussion of the ADA's coverage of the Internet see CRS Report R40462, *The Americans with Disabilities Act: Application to the Internet*, by Nancy Lee Jones.

[8] Arizona v. Harkins Amusement Enterprises, 603 F.3d 666 (9th Cir. 2010).

[9] 42 U.S.C. §12182.

[10] 42 U.S.C. §12181(7)(C).

[11] 42 U.S.C. §12182(b)(1)(A)(ii).

[12] 42 U.S.C. §12182(b)(2)(A)(iii).

[13] 42 U.S.C. §12103.

[14] 28 C.F.R. §36.104 (2010). The factors to be considered are the nature and cost of the action needed; the overall financial resources of the site or sites involved, including legitimate safety requirements; the geographic separateness and the administrative or fiscal relationship of the site to any parent corporation; if applicable, the overall financial resources of any parent corporation; and if applicable, the type of operation of any parent corporation.

[15] H.Rept. 101-485 (II) at 108 (1990)(Report of the House Education and Labor Committee); H.Rept. 101-485 (III) at 59 (Report of the House Judiciary Committee); S. Rept. 101-116 at 64 (1989)(Report of the Senate Committee on Labor and Human Resources). Open captioning is similar to subtitles since the text of dialogue is visible to all but, unlike subtitles, it includes descriptions of other sounds as well.

[16] H.Rept. 101-485 (II) at 108 (1990)(Report of the House Education and Labor Committee).

[17] 75 FED. REG. 43470 (July 26, 2010).

[18] 75 FED. REG. 56164 (September 15, 2010).

[19] 75 FED. REG. 43471 (July 26, 2010).

[20] *Id.* at 43374-43476.

[21] 603 F.3d 666 (9th Cir. 2010).

[22] *Id.* at 670.

[23] *Id.* at 671 quoting 42 U.S.C. §12182(b)(2)(A)(iii).

[24] *Id.* at 674.

[25] 75 FED. REG. 43469 (July 26, 2010).

In: The Americans with Disabilities Act (ADA): Provisions...   ISBN: 978-1-61470-961-9
Editor: John Kiviniemi and Cécile Sanjo   © 2012 Nova Science Publishers, Inc.

Chapter 11

THE AMERICANS WITH DISABILITIES ACT (ADA) AND SERVICE ANIMALS

Nancy Lee Jones

SUMMARY

The Americans with Disabilities Act (ADA) has as its purpose providing "a clear and comprehensive national mandate for the elimination of discrimination against individuals with disabilities." In order to effectuate this purpose, the ADA and its regulations require reasonable accommodation or modifications in policies, practices, or procedures when such modifications are necessary to render the goods, services, facilities, privileges, advantages, or accommodations accessible to individuals with disabilities. The reasonable accommodation or modification requirement has been interpreted to allow the use of service animals, even in places where animals are generally not permitted.

The Department of Justice (DOJ) has promulgated regulations containing specific details about service animals, and this report focuses on these regulatory requirements. Generally, a public entity (ADA title II) or a place of public accommodation (ADA title III) must modify its policies, practices, and procedures to allow an individual with a disability to use a service animal. The regulations also define service animals. A service animal is "any **dog** that is individually trained to do work or perform tasks for the benefit of an individual with a disability, including a physical, sensory, psychiatric, intellectual, or other mental disability." (emphasis added). However, despite the regulatory limitation of the definition to dogs, miniature horses may be allowed in certain circumstances. A service animal does not need to be allowed when the animal is out of control or the animal is not housebroken. In addition, a public entity or place of public accommodation may not ask about the nature or extent of an individual's disability but may ask two questions to determine if the animal is a service animal when it is not readily apparent. These questions are, if the animal is required because of a disability, and what work or task the animal is trained to do.

Several issues remain unresolved by the DOJ regulations. For example, the relationship between the ADA and Fair Housing Act in some situations is unclear. In addition, there is considerable ambiguity concerning how potentially conflicting claims for accommodations relating to service animals should be addressed.

INTRODUCTION

The Americans with Disabilities Act (ADA)[1] has often been described as the most sweeping nondiscrimination legislation since the Civil Rights Act of 1964. It provides broad nondiscrimination protection in employment, public services, public accommodations, and services operated by private entities, transportation, and telecommunications for individuals with disabilities. As stated in the act, its purpose is "to provide a clear and comprehensive national mandate for the elimination of discrimination against individuals with disabilities."[2]

The ADA and its regulations require reasonable accommodation or modifications in policies, practices, or procedures when such modifications are necessary to render the goods, services, facilities, privileges, advantages, or accommodations accessible to individuals with disabilities. This concept is found in title I, regarding employment,[3] title II, regarding public entities,[4] and title III, regarding public accommodations.[5] The reasonable accommodation or modification requirement has been interpreted to allow the use of service animals, even in places where animals are generally not permitted. Recently, the Department of Justice (DOJ) promulgated regulations containing specific details about service animals, including when they may be denied access, and defining service animals as trained dogs.[6] This report focuses on these regulatory requirements.

DEFINITION OF SERVICE ANIMAL

Species Limitation

Currently, the DOJ regulations for titles II and III of the ADA define service animal as "any **dog** that is individually trained to do work or perform tasks for the benefit of an individual with a disability, including a physical, sensory, psychiatric, intellectual, or other mental disability."[7] Previously, the DOJ regulations had defined service animal as a dog or other animal individually trained to do work or perform tasks for the benefit of an individual with a disability;[8] however, the variety of animal species promoted as service animals led to DOJ's limitation of the definition. The regulations specifically exclude other species of animals whether or not they are wild or domestic or trained or untrained.[9] DOJ notes that, at the time of the promulgation of the original regulations, "few anticipated the variety of animals that would be promoted as service animals in the years to come, which ranged from pigs, and miniature horses to snakes, iguanas, and parrots."[10] Arguments were made by commentators on the proposed regulations for the inclusion of monkeys, particularly capuchin monkeys, who were trained to provide in-home services to individuals with paraplegia and quadriplegia. However, DOJ rejected these arguments noting the potential for disease transmission and unpredictable aggressive behavior.[11]

Work or Tasks Performed by Service Animals

The DOJ regulations specifically define a service animal as "any dog that is individually trained **to do work or perform tasks** for the benefit of an individual with a disability."[12] The regulations elaborate on the meaning of this requirement mandating that the "work or tasks performed by a service animal must be directly related to the handler's disability."[13] Examples of work or tasks are provided and include the following:

- Assisting individuals who are blind or have low vision with navigation
- Alerting individuals who are deaf or hard of hearing to the presence of people or sounds
- Providing non-violent protection or rescue work
- Pulling a wheelchair
- Assisting an individual during a seizure
- Alerting individuals to the presence of allergens
- Retrieving items such as medicine or the telephone
- Providing physical support and assistance with balance to individuals with mobility disabilities
- Helping individuals with psychiatric and neurological disabilities by preventing or interrupting impulsive or destructive behaviors[14]

However, the fact that the presence of an animal may deter crime or provide emotional support does not constitute work or a task.[15] DOJ emphasizes the importance of the concept of doing work or performing tasks and states that "unless the animal is individually trained to do something that qualifies as work or a task, the animal is a pet or support animal and does not qualify for coverage as a service animal."[16] The process for determining if an animal is doing work or performing a task is described as two-part: first, the animal must recognize the problem, and second, the animal must respond. An example would be recognition by a service animal that a person is about to have a psychiatric episode, and a response to this recognition by nudging, barking, or removing the individual to a safe location.[17]

Whether or not to include "comfort animals" in the definition of service animals was controversial. DOJ recognizes that the Fair Housing Act (FHA)[18] and the Air Carriers Access Act (ACAA)[19] may create legal obligations for an entity to allow a comfort animal and that this difference from the ADA requirements could lead to confusion.[20] However, DOJ notes that its distinction between a service animal and a comfort animal is based on differences in the covered entities; ADA titles II and III govern a broader range of public settings than either the FHA or the ACAA.

Miniature Horses

Despite the regulatory limitation in the definition to dogs, miniature horses may be allowed in certain circumstances. Although they are not included in the definition of service animal, the regulations specifically provide that a public entity (title II) or public accommodation (title III) "shall make reasonable modifications in policies, practices, or procedures to permit the use of a miniature horse by an individual with a disability if the miniature horse has been individually trained to do work or perform tasks for the benefit of the individual with a disability."[21] DOJ notes that this provision for miniature horses was made since miniature horses are a viable alternative to dogs for individuals with allergies or who have religious beliefs that preclude the use of dogs. In addition, the longer life span of miniature horses reduces the replacement cost of an animal.[22]

In order to determine whether the modifications required for a miniature horse are "reasonable," the regulations provide that public entities or public accommodations shall consider four factors:

- The type, size, and weight of the miniature horse and whether the facility can accommodate these features
- Whether the handler has sufficient control over the miniature horse
- Whether the miniature horse is house broken
- Whether the miniature horse's presence compromises legitimate safety requirements[23]

The specific times when a service animal may be properly excluded,[24] discussed *infra,* are applicable to miniature horses. In addition, ponies and full sized horses are not covered and miniature horses may be excluded if their presence results in "a fundamental alteration to the nature of the programs, activities, or services provided."[25]

REQUIRED MODIFICATION OF POLICIES, PRACTICES, AND PROCEDURES AND EXCEPTIONS

Generally, a public entity (title II) or a place of public accommodation (title III) must modify its policies, practices, and procedures to allow an individual with a disability to use a service animal.[26] More specifically, individuals with disabilities must be permitted to be accompanied by their service animal in areas where other members of the public, or participants in programs or activities are allowed.[27] A public entity or place of public accommodation may not ask or require a surcharge for a service animal, even if people with pets must pay an additional fee.[28]

However, there are certain limitations on these requirements, and, as noted previously, these limitations also apply to miniature horses. The animal must be under its handler's control and the public entity or place of public accommodation is not responsible for the care or supervision of the animal.[29] The regulations specifically allow a public entity or a place of public accommodation to ask an individual with a disability to remove a service animal from the premises when

- the animal is out of control and its handler does not take effective action to control it, or
- the animal is not housebroken.[30]

In its discussion of these exceptions, DOJ observes that an animal may misbehave when provoked or injured. If there is reason to suspect this has occurred, a public entity or a place of public accommodation should determine the facts and, if provocation or injury has occurred, take steps to prevent any similar actions.[31] When the service animal is properly excluded, the public entity or a place of public accommodation must give the individual with a disability the opportunity to participate in the service, program, or activity without the animal.[32]

A public entity or place of public accommodation may not ask about the nature or extent of an individual's disability but may ask two questions to determine if the animal is a service animal, when it is not readily apparent. These two questions are

- if the animal is required because of a disability, and
- what work or task the animal is trained to do.[33]

OTHER ISSUES RELATING TO SERVICE ANIMALS

Although the DOJ title II and III regulations provide significant guidance regarding service animals, there are still some issues remaining. For example, the exact interaction between the ADA's requirements and those of other statutes, such as the Fair Housing Act, is somewhat uncertain. When a facility has a mixed use—such as a hotel which allows both residential and short-term stays but does not allocate space for these different uses in separate, discrete units—both the ADA and the Fair Housing Act may apply to the facility.[34] Exactly how the differing service animal requirements would apply in this situation is unclear and will most likely await judicial determinations.

Similarly, DOJ regulations do not address the issues involved when an individual with allergies to dogs and an individual with a disability using a service animal both attempt to use a place of public accommodation. This situation, which may occur more often given the more expansive definition of disability provided in ADA Amendments Act,[35] was at issue in *Lockett v. Catalina Channel Express, Inc.*[36] In *Lockett,* Catalina Channel Express (CCE), which operates a ferry between Long Beach and Catalina Island, instituted a policy of excluding animals from part of the ferry because of a request by a frequent passenger for an area free of animal dander. When an individual with a visual impairment and a guide dog attempted to buy a ticket for this part of the ferry, the CCE refused, although it changed its policy two weeks later. The court of appeals found that the CCE had made a "one-time reasonable judgment … while it investigated the competing interests" and emphasized the narrowness of its holding. Thus, there is considerable ambiguity concerning how potentially conflicting claims for accommodations relating to service animals should be addressed.

End Notes

[1] 42 U.S.C. §§12101 et seq. For a more detailed discussion of the ADA see CRS Report 98-921, *The Americans with Disabilities Act (ADA): Statutory Language and Recent Issues*, by Nancy Lee Jones.
[2] 42 U.S.C. §12101(b)(1).

[3] 42 U.S.C. §12111(9)(defining reasonable accommodation); 42 U.S.C. §12112(b)(5)(discrimination defined as not making a reasonable accommodation unless the covered entity can demonstrate that the accommodation would impose an undue hardship).

[4] 28 C.F.R. §130(b)(7).

[5] 42 U.S.C. §12182(b)(2)(A)(ii).

[6] 75 FED. REG. 56164 (September 15, 2010) (title II); 75 FED. REG. 56236 (September 15, 2010) (title III). For a discussion of the changes made by these new regulations see CRS Report R41376, *The Americans with Disabilities Act (ADA): Final Rule Amending Title II and Title III Regulations*, by Nancy Lee Jones.

[7] 35 C.F.R. §35.104, 75 FED. REG. 56177 (September 15, 2010) (title II); 36 C.F.R. §36.104, 75 FED. REG. 56250 (September 15, 2010) (title III)(emphasis added).

[8] 28 C.F.R. §36.104 (July 1, 2010)(title III). Previously, title II had no specific language regarding service animals but DOJ had interpreted title II as having the same service animal requirements as title III. 75 FED. REG. 56191 (September 15, 2010).

[9] 35 C.F.R. §35.104, 75 FED. REG. 56177 (September 15, 2010) (title II); 36 C.F.R. §36.104, 75 FED. REG. 56250 (September 15, 2010) (title III).

[10] 75 FED. REG. 56193 (September 15, 2010)(title II); 75 FED. REG. 56267 (September 15, 2010)(title III).

[11] 75 FED. REG. . 56194 (September 15, 2010) (title II); 75 FED. REG. 56267 (September 15, 2010) (title III).

[12] 35 C.F.R. §35.104, 75 FED. REG. 56177 (September 15, 2010) (title II); 36 C.F.R. §36.104, 75 FED. REG. 56250 (September 15, 2010) (title III)(emphasis added).

[13] *Id.*

[14] *Id.*

[15] *Id.*

[16] 75 FED. REG. 56193 (September 15, 2010)(title II); 75 FED. REG. 56267 (September 15, 2010)(title III).

[17] *Id.*

[18] 42 U.S.C. §§3601 *et seq.* For a general discussion of this law see CRS Report 95-710, *The Fair Housing Act (FHA): A Legal Overview*, by Todd Garvey.

[19] 49 U.S.C. §§41705 *et seq.* For a general discussion of this law see CRS Report RL34047, *Overview of the Air Carrier Access Act (ACAA)*, by Emily C. Barbour.

[20] 75 FED. REG. 56195 (September 15, 2010)(title II); 75 FED. REG. 56269 (September 15, 2010)(title III).

[21] 35 C.F.R. §35.136(i) 75 FED. REG. 56178 (September 15, 2010) (title II); 36 C.F.R. §36.302(c)(9), 75 FED. REG. 56251 (September 15, 2010) (title III).

[22] 75 FED. REG. 56198 (September 15, 2010)(title II); 75 FED. REG. 56272 (September 15, 2010)(title III).

[23] *Id.*

[24] 35 C.F.R. §35.136(c)-(h) 75 FED. REG. 56178 (September 15, 2010) (title II); 36 C.F.R. §36.302(c)(3)-(8), 75 FED. REG. 56251 (September 15, 2010) (title III).

[25] 75 FED. REG. 56199 (September 15, 2010)(title II); 75 FED. REG. 56273 (September 15, 2010)(title III).

[26] 35 C.F.R. §35.136(a) 7FED. REG. FED. REG. . 56178 (September 15, 2010) (title II); 36 C.F.R. §36.302(c)(1), 75 FED. REG. REG. 56251 (September 15, 2010) (title III).

[27] 35 C.F.R. §35.136(g) 75 FED. REG. 56178 (September 15, 2010) (title II); 36 C.F.R. §36.302(c)(7), 75 FED. REG. FED. REG. 56251 (September 15, 2010) (title III).

[28] 35 C.F.R. §35.136(h) 75 FED. REG. 56178 (September 15, 2010) (title II); 36 C.F.R. §36.302(c)(8), 75 FED. REG. FED. REG. 56251 (September 15, 2010) (title III).

[29] 35 C.F.R. §35.136(d)-(e), 75 FED. REG. 56178 (September 15, 2010) (title II); 36 C.F.R. §36.302(c)(4)-(5), 75 FED. REG. 56251 (September 15, 2010) (title III).

[30] 35 C.F.R. §35.136(b) 75 FED. REG. 56178 (September 15, 2010) (title II); 36 C.F.R. §36.302(c)(2), 75 FED. REG. FED. REG. 56251 (September 15, 2010) (title III).

[31] 75 FED. REG. 56197 (September 15, 2010)(title II); 75 FED. REG. 56272 (September 15, 2010)(title III).

[32] 35 C.F.R. §35.136(c) 75 FED. REG. 56178 (September 15, 2010) (title II); 36 C.F.R. §36.302(c)(3), 75 FED. REG. FED. REG. 56251 (September 15, 2010) (title III).

[33] 35 C.F.R. §35.136(f) 75 FED. REG. 56178 (September 15, 2010) (title II); 36 C.F.R. §36.302(c)(6), 75 FED. REG. FED. REG. 56251 (September 15, 2010) (title III).

[34] 56 Fed. Reg. 35,552 (July 26, 1991).

[35] For a more detailed discussion of this act see, CRS Report RL34691, *The ADA Amendments Act: P.L. 110-325*, by Nancy Lee Jones.

[36] 496 F.3d 1061 (9th Cir. 2007).

In: The Americans with Disabilities Act (ADA): Provisions…   ISBN: 978-1-61470-961-9
Editor: John Kiviniemi and Cécile Sanjo   © 2012 Nova Science Publishers, Inc.

Chapter 12

PUBLIC TRANSPORTATION PROVIDERS' OBLIGATIONS UNDER THE AMERICANS WITH DISABILITIES ACT (ADA)

Carol J. Toland

SUMMARY

The Americans with Disabilities Act (ADA) has as its purpose providing "a clear and comprehensive national mandate for the elimination of discrimination against individuals with disabilities." In order to effectuate this purpose, the ADA and its regulations require reasonable accommodation or modifications in policies, practices, or procedures when such modifications are necessary to render the goods, services, facilities, privileges, advantages, or accommodations accessible to individuals with disabilities. The reasonable accommodation or modification requirement has been interpreted to allow the use of service animals, even in places where animals are generally not permitted.

STATUTORY LANGUAGE

Under the ADA, individuals with disabilities may not "be excluded from participation in or be denied the benefits of the services, programs, or activities of a public entity, or be subjected to discrimination by any such entity."[1] In the context of public transportation, the statute requires transportation entities to offer supplemental "paratransit" service for people with disabilities. The statute provides,

> it shall be considered discrimination . . . for a public entity which operates a fixed route system . . . to fail to provide . . . paratransit [services] . . . that are sufficient to provide to such individuals a level of service (1) which is comparable to the level of designated public transportation services provided to individuals without disabilities using such system; or (2) in the case of response time, which is comparable, to the extent practicable, to the level of designated public transportation services provided to individuals without disabilities using such system.[2]

All public entities operating a "fixed-route system" are subject to the ADA's complementary paratransit requirements. The ADA defines "fixed-route system" as "a system of providing designated public transportation on which a vehicle is operated along a prescribed route according to a fixed schedule."[3]

A public entity is any state or local government, any department or instrumentality of a state or local government, the National Railroad Passenger Corporation, and certain commuter authorities.[4] Also, the subcontractors of such public entities are subject to these obligations, even if the subcontractors are private entities.[5]

PARATRANSIT REGULATIONS

The Department of Transportation first promulgated regulations to implement the ADA's public transportation provisions on September 6, 1991.[6] Under these regulations, "each public entity operating a fixed route system" (excluding commuter bus, commuter rail, and intercity rail systems) must provide "comparable" paratransit service for individuals with disabilities.[7] Paratransit service, generally defined, is responsive, accessible origin-to-destination transportation service that is an alternative to a fixed-route system.

It is important to note that paratransit requirements do not authorize public entities to supercede the ADA's other non-discrimination provisions. Although the regulations obligate entities to offer paratransit service, the regulations also forbid entities from *requiring* their customers with disabilities to utilize the paratransit services instead of the services available to the general public. Specifically, transportation entities "shall not, on the basis of disability, deny to any individual with a disability the opportunity to use the entity's transportation service for the general public, if the individual is capable of using that service."[8] Furthermore, entities shall not require that individuals with disabilities sit in specific seats[9] or be accompanied by an attendant.[10]

MINIMUM SERVICE REQUIREMENTS

The statutory language provides little guidance regarding the required scope of paratransit service. It merely requires entities to offer a level of service that is "comparable" to the level of service offered to the general public.[11] The ADA therefore required the Department of Transportation to develop minimum service criteria to "determine the level of services" sufficient to be "comparable" with services offered to individuals without disabilities.[12] Note that the regulations do not prohibit public entities from offering paratransit services that exceed these minimum service requirements.[13]

Eligibility

The regulations require entities to provide paratransit service to all "paratransit-eligible" individuals,[14] including non-resident visitors "who present documentation that they are ADA paratransit eligible."[15] An individual is paratransit-eligible if he or she is an individual with a disability who meets the requirements for one of three categories. The first eligibility category includes individuals who are unable, as a result of a physical or mental impairment, to board and ride accessible fixed-route transit systems.[16] Department commentary accompanying the final rule shows that the department intended this first category to especially target individuals who are unable to "navigate the system."[17] The second eligibility category includes individuals who are able to use accessible vehicles but whose fixed-route system lacks accessible vehicles.[18] Finally, the third eligibility category includes individuals "who ... [have] specific impairment-related condition[s] which ... prevent[s] such individual[s] from traveling to a boarding location or from a disembarking location on such system."[19]

The regulations also require entities to provide paratransit service to one individual accompanying each paratransit-eligible individual.[20] This accompanying-individual allowance does not address assistance by personal care attendants; rather, it enables individuals with disabilities to travel with a friend or family member for pleasure. Thus, if the individual with a disability requires a personal care attendant, an accompanying individual shall also be provided service.[21]

Service Times

The regulation regarding minimum service times implements the ADA's "comparable" requirement in a straightforward manner. It provides that public entities must offer paratransit services for the same time frame for which they offer fixed-route transportation service to the general public.[22]

Fares

The regulations allow entities to charge a higher fare to paratransit riders than they charge to general riders; however, the fare charged to paratransit riders cannot exceed twice the amount charged to an individual for a similar trip on the general, fixed-route transportation service.[23] Likewise, the entity cannot charge "premiums" above this amount unless the premium is charged for services that exceed the minimum service requirements mandated by the regulations.[24]

Geographic Scope

Under the regulations, entities must provide paratransit service in all areas within three quarters of a mile of the fixed-route service.[25] For bus systems, this requirement refers to three-quarters of a mile on either side of the fixed-route corridor and includes "small areas not inside any of the corridors but which are surrounded by corridors."[26] For rail systems, this requirement refers to a three-quarter-mile radius surrounding each rail station.[27]

"Origin to Destination"

The regulations require that all paratransit service be "origin-to-destination" service.[28] The department intentionally left ambiguous whether "origin-to-destination" service means door-to-door or curb-to-curb service, preferring to leave that specific "operational decision" to local-level decision-makers.[29] However, in later guidance documents, the department has clarified that it would be inappropriate for an entity to "establish an inflexible policy that refuses to provide service to eligible passengers beyond the curb in all circumstances."[30]

Response Times

Multiple regulations govern entities' obligations regarding the time it takes to respond to an individual's request for paratransit service. One response-time regulation, the next-day service requirement, provides a bright-line rule: it requires transportation entities to provide paratransit services for the day after a paratransit-eligible person has requested them.[31] That regulation further states that, although entities can negotiate pick-up times, they cannot move the requested time by more than one hour.[32] A second Department of Transportation regulation, which governs "capacity constraints," seems to allow for flexibility in the next-day service provision requirement. It provides an exclusive list of ways in which entities cannot limit the availability of complementary paratransit service, thereby suggesting that other manners of limiting the service are acceptable. Specifically, this "capacity constraints" regulation prohibits limiting paratransit service in any of the following ways: "(1) [r]estrictions on the number of trips an individual will be provided; (2) [w]aiting lists for access to the service; or (3) [a]ny operational pattern or practice that significantly limits the availability of service to ADA paratransit eligible persons."[33] This regulation also provides examples of discriminatory "patterns or practices," including "(A) [s]ubstantial numbers of significantly untimely pickups for initial or return trips; (B) [s]ubstantial numbers of trip denials or missed trips; [and] (C) [s]ubstantial numbers of trips with excessive trip lengths."[34]

At least one court has interpreted the department's multiple regulations regarding paratransit response times as being somewhat in tension.[35] In *Anderson v. Rochester-Genesee Regional Transportation Authority*, the Second Circuit—relying on Department of Transportation commentary accompanying these regulations, an agency opinion letter addressed to the court, and opinion letters issued by the Federal Transit Administration's Office of Civil Rights—interpreted the next-day service requirement (49 C.F.R. §37.131(b)) as imposing an affirmative obligation on public entities to plan, design, and implement a paratransit service that meets 100% of demand and accounts for fluctuations in demand over time.[36] Additionally, it interpreted the more flexible "capacity constraints" regulation as functioning to give entities practical flexibility when situations arise for which advance planning is difficult.[37] Therefore, the court held that a transportation provider cannot be held liable for failing to meet 100% of demand for paratransit services unless the failure results in denying a number of paratransit-eligible riders "sufficient to constitute a pattern or practice."[38]

In *Anderson*, plaintiffs argued that the Rochester Genesee Regional Transportation Authority (RGRTA), a public entity for purposes of the ADA, violated the ADA when it denied them and other disabled riders paratransit services scheduled a day or more in advance.[39] RGRTA admitted denying rides requested a day or more in advance by paratransit-eligible riders but claimed that it denied the rides because it encountered "not unusual" constraints on capacity.[40] The court held that RGRTA had violated the ADA because RGRTA's organizational records showed that RGRTA had anticipated an increased demand for paratransit services and yet failed to plan or change its operations in order to meet that demand.

Similarly, in *Martin v Metropolitan Atlanta Rapid Transit Authority*, plaintiffs sued the Metropolitan Atlanta Mass Transit Authority (MARTA), alleging in part that MARTA discriminated against riders with disabilities by failing to provide adequate paratransit service.[41] The *Martin* court held that the plaintiffs had a substantial likelihood on the success of the merits for their paratransit claim, because "operational patterns and practices in MARTA's paratransit service [had] significantly limited the availability of service to paratransit eligible persons in violation of the ADA."[42] According to the court, MARTA's troubling practices included changing "ready times" without properly notifying riders and charging riders for paratransit service even when the driver arrived more than thirty minutes after the scheduled "ready time."

In sum, the available case law interpreting the paratransit response time regulations appears to suggest that under the next-day service requirement entities must plan to meet 100% of demand for next-day service to paratransit riders. However, the case law also suggests that under the capacity constraints regulation entities can be held liable for failing to provide next-day service only if such a failure results in one of the three situations—waiting lists, restricting rides for an individual person, or a discriminatory "pattern or practice"—as enumerated in 49 C.F.R. §37.131(f).

UNDUE BURDEN EXCEPTION

The ADA limits its paratransit requirement by waiving the obligation in cases where providing such a service would impose an "undue financial burden" on an entity.[43] The regulations delineate 10 factors for the Federal Transit Administration to consider when determining whether an entity is entitled to an "undue burden" waiver.[44] These include (1) "[e]ffects on current fixed route service," (2) average number of per capita trips made by the general population as compared with the average number of per capita trips made by paratransit riders, (3) "[r]eductions in other services," (4) "[i]ncreases in fares," (5) "[r]esources available to implement complementary paratransit service," (6) "[p]ercentage of budget needed to implement the plan," (7) "current level of accessible service," (8) "[c]ooperation/coordination among area transportation providers," (9) "[e]vidence of increased efficiencies," and (10) unique circumstances in the area.[45]

ACKNOWLEDGMENTS

This report originally was prepared by Anna C. Henning, Law Clerk.

End Notes

[1] 42 U.S.C. § 12132 (2009).

[2] 42 U.S.C. § 12143(a) (2009).

[3] 42 U.S.C. § 12141(3) (2009).

[4] 42 U.S.C. § 12131(1) (2009).

[5] ADA regulations allow public entities to contract with private entities to provide fixed route services. 49 C.F.R. § 37.23(a) (2010). When they enter such a contract, however, public entities must ensure that the private entities adhere to ADA regulations, including requirements for paratransit services. For more information on subcontractors' requirements, see http://www.fta.dot.gov/civilrights/ada/civil_rights_3892.html.

[6] 56 Fed. Reg. 45584 *et seq.*

[7] 49 C.F.R. §§ 37.121(a), (c) (2010).

[8] 49 C.F.R. § 37.5(b) (2010).

[9] 49 C.F.R. § 37.5(c) (2010).

[10] 49 C.F.R. § 37.5(e) (2010).

[11] 42 U.S.C. § 12143(a) (2009).

[12] 42 U.S.C. § 12143(b) (2009).

[13] 49 C.F.R. § 37.131(g) (2010).

[14] 49 C.F.R. § 37.123(a) (2010).

[15] 49 C.F.R. § 37.127(c) (2010).

[16] 49 C.F.R. § 37.123(e)(1) (2010).

[17] 56 Fed. Reg. 45601.

[18] 49 C.F.R. § 37.123(e)(2) (2010).

[19] 49 C.F.R. § 37.123(e)(3) (2010). *See also* 56 Fed. Reg. 45602.

[20] 49 C.F.R. § 37.123(f)(1) (2010).

[21] 49 C.F.R. § 37.123(f)(1)(i) (2010).

[22] 49 C.F.R. § 37.131(e) (2010).

[23] 49 C.F.R. § 37.131(c) (2010).

[24] For more information about charging premiums for paratransit service, see http://www.fta.dot.gov/civilrights/ada/civil_rights_3895.html.

[25] 49 C.F.R. § 37.131(a) (2010).

[26] 49 C.F.R. § 37.131(a)(1) (2010).

[27] 49 C.F.R. § 37.131(a)(2)(i) (2010).

[28] 49 C.F.R. § 37.129(a) (2010).

[29] 56 Fed. Reg. 45604.

[30] http://www.fta.dot.gov/civilrights/ada/civil_rights_3891.html.

[31] 49 C.F.R. § 37.131(b) (2010).

[32] 49 C.F.R. § 37.131(b)(2) (2010).

[33] 49 C.F.R. § 37.131(f) (2010).

[34] 49 C.F.R. § 37.131(f)(3)(i) (2010).

[35] *See* Anderson v. Rochester-Genesee Regional Transportation Authority, 337 F.3d 201, 207 (2d Cir. 2003).

[36] *Id.* at 208.

[37] *Id.* at 212.

[38] *Id.*

[39] *Id.* at 204.

[40] *Id* at 213.

[41] 225 F.Supp.2d 1362, 1371 (N.D. GA 2002).

[42] *Id.* at 1380.

[43] 42 U.S.C. 12143(c)(4) (2009).

[44] 49 C.F.R. § 37.155(a) (2010).

[45] *Id.*

In: The Americans with Disabilities Act (ADA): Provisions...   ISBN: 978-1-61470-961-9
Editor: John Kiviniemi and Cécile Sanjo   © 2012 Nova Science Publishers, Inc.

Chapter 13

FEDERAL LAW ON PARKING PRIVILEGES FOR PERSONS WITH DISABILITIES

Carol J. Toland

SUMMARY

State law generally governs parking privileges for people with disabilities. However, federal regulations offer a uniform system of parking privileges, which includes model definitions and rules regarding license plates and placards, parking and parking space design, and interstate reciprocity. The federal government encourages states to adopt this uniform system. As a result, most states have incorporated at least some aspects of the uniform regulations into their handicapped parking laws. This report describes the federal role in parking privileges law, outlines the uniform system's model rules, and briefly discusses state responses to the model federal rules.

FEDERAL ROLE

Parking privileges for individuals with disabilities is distinct from the subject of physical accessibility of parking spaces or structures. The federal role in ensuring physical parking space accessibility is significant: under the Americans with Disabilities Act (ADA), a broad nondiscrimination statute,[1] government entities, private businesses, and others[2] must adhere to the ADA Standards for Accessible Design when re-striping existing or building new parking lots.[3] The ADA standards mandate specific percentages of van-accessible parking spaces per parking facility and require accessible aisles between certain spaces.[4] However, the ADA Standards for Accessible Design do not require governments or other entities to reserve accessible parking spaces or issue special license plates or placards for individuals with disabilities; nor does any other ADA regulation mandate the provision of such parking privileges. Therefore, any federal action on parking privileges occurs separately from federal rules on physical parking space accessibility.

Congress first considered federal action on parking privileges for individuals with disabilities in the mid-1980s in response to complaints that some states did not honor parking placards for individuals with disabilities from other states. The first bills introduced during that period would have created federal guidelines and authorized penalties for states that failed to comply with those guidelines. Specifically, the initial bills proposed federal sanctions in the form of reduced highway apportionments for states that failed to recognize parking placards issued by other states or failed to implement federal rules.[5] However, those early proposals were not reported out of their respective committees.

Since that time, the federal government has created guidelines for parking privileges. In 1988, Congress enacted legislation requiring the Department of Transportation to create a "uniform system" of parking privileges for people with disabilities.[6] Accordingly, the Department of Transportation promulgated the "Uniform System for Parking for Persons with Disabilities."[7]

However, Congress has never required states to comply with the Uniform System, nor has it authorized penalties for non-complying states.[8] Rather, the enacted law and resulting federal guidelines are merely hortatory.[9] The legislation required the department to "encourage adoption of such system by all the states,"[10] but it did not require states to adopt the federal guidelines. Thus, although the federal government has a strong advisory role, states have the ultimate responsibility for the development of parking privileges.

THE UNIFORM SYSTEM

The stated purpose of the Department of Transportation's Uniform System for Parking for Persons with Disabilities is to provide "guidelines to States for the establishment of a uniform system."[11] Thus, the Uniform System provides model definitions and rules regarding eligibility, application procedures, and issuance of special license plates and placards. It also contains information to aid states in developing reciprocal systems of parking privileges, including sample placards and a model rule regarding reciprocity.

The Uniform System is brief. It does not contain model rules regarding enforcement, nor does it provide model rules specifying lengths of time after which special plates or placards must be renewed or addressing whether eligible individuals must be primary users of vehicles with special license plates. Instead, it contains basic definitions and samples that the department encourages states to utilize as part of their own, more detailed, parking privilege systems.

Eligibility

One key provision in the Uniform System is the model definition of eligible individuals. Unlike the ADA, which protects every individual with a "disability,"[12] the Uniform System extends parking privileges only to "persons with disabilities which impair or limit the ability to walk."[13] This definition includes people who (1) "[c]annot walk 200 feet without stopping to rest"; (2) cannot walk without the aid of another person or certain assistive devices; (3) have respiratory volumes of less than a certain amount due to lung disease; (4) "[u]se portable oxygen"; (5) have cardiac conditions of a specified severity; or (6) "[a]re severely limited in their ability to walk due to an arthritic, neurological, or orthopedic condition."[14] Under the Uniform System, individuals' fit within any of these categories must be "determined by a licensed physician."[15]

Application Process

If an individual qualifies as a person with a disability which impairs or limits his or her ability to walk, then under the Uniform System's model rules, he or she may submit an application for special license plates[16] or a windshield placard, which entitle the individual to park in specially reserved parking spaces.[17] A certification from a licensed physician must accompany an initial application for such plates and placards.[18] Under the Uniform System guidelines, states may not charge a higher fee for special license plates than they charge for regular license plates.[19]

Placards

Together with special license plates, placards "shall be the only recognized means of identifying vehicles permitted to utilize parking spaces reserved for persons with disabilities which limit or impair the ability to walk" under the Uniform System.[20] The system delineates two types of windshield placards: removable windshield placards and temporary removable windshield placards. Removable windshield placards are appropriate for individuals who will qualify as persons with disabilities which impair or limit the ability to walk permanently or for at least six months. Temporary removable windshield placards are most appropriate for individuals who will have such an impairment or limitation for less than six months.[21]

The Uniform System provides samples of each type of windshield placard.[22] The sample placards display the "International Symbol of Access," which was adopted by the disability rights organization Rehabilitation International in 1969.[23] The symbol is a commonly recognized image of a wheelchair and is best known as a white chair on a blue background. The samples also include spaces in which to display names of issuing authorities and expiration dates for the placards.[24]

Reciprocity

In addition to sample placards, which aid efforts for reciprocity among states indirectly by providing a commonly recognized symbol, the Uniform System includes a model rule that directly addresses reciprocity. It provides that states "shall recognize removable windshield placards, temporary removable windshield placards and special license plates which have been issued by issuing authorities of other States and countries."[25]

State Responses

All states have laws governing parking privileges for individuals with disabilities, and nearly all states have adopted at least some portion of the Department of Transportation's Uniform System. Most states extend privileges to visitors with placards issued by other states. Also, most states issue placards closely resembling the Uniform System's sample placard.[26] However, other aspects of the state systems vary greatly.

Eligibility

Regarding eligibility, some states have incorporated the Uniform System's definition of an individual with a disability which limits or impairs the ability to walk word-for-word into their eligibility criteria.[27] Other states' eligibility criteria are entirely distinct from the Uniform System definition.[28] Between these two options, most states have incorporated the Uniform System's definition in their statutes but have modified or expanded it. For example, some states have added a category for blindness to the Uniform System definition.[29]

Reciprocity

Most states extend parking privileges to individuals with special license plates or placards issued by other states. Many states even extend privileges to people with placards issued by other countries.[30] The language in these reciprocity provisions differs from state to state. Some states codified most or all of the Uniform System's reciprocity provision.[31] Other states adopted little or no language from the Uniform System but recognize out-of-state placards nonetheless.[32] A few states extend conditional privileges to out-of-state visitors; for example, North Dakota extends privileges only to people from states that also extend privileges to traveling North Dakotans.[33]

However, even states that extend parking privileges to out-of-state visitors have rules that out-of-state visitors might not know to follow. For example, Iowa requires that placards be displayed only when individuals with disabilities are actually utilizing reserved parking spaces.[34]

Application Process and Administration

The state laws are fairly similar regarding some application procedures and criteria for which the Uniform System provides model rules. For example, most states require eligible individuals to apply for both special license plates and either temporary or more permanent windshield placards. Likewise, most states issue special license plates or placards after receipt of an application containing certification by a physician, as the Uniform System suggests.

In contrast, states' laws are relatively different regarding administrative aspects of parking privileges that the Uniform System does not address. For example, state rules regarding the duration for which removable windshield placards will be valid—an aspect the Uniform System does not address—vary from just two years to indefinitely.[35]

In sum, the Department of Transportation's Uniform System has increased uniformity in the state laws. Many states utilize uniform sample placards and have enacted statutes requiring reciprocal privileges for individuals bearing placards issued by other states. Nonetheless, the state systems differ in many aspects of parking privilege administration.

ACKNOWLEDGMENTS

This report originally was prepared by Anna Henning, Law Clerk, American Law Division.

End Notes

[1] 42 U.S.C. §§ 12101 *et. seq.* For a discussion of the ADA, see CRS Report 98-921, *The Americans with Disabilities Act (ADA): Statutory Language and Recent Issues*, by Nancy Lee Jones.

[2] This requirement applies to public entities and all places of "public accommodation" as defined under the ADA. *See* 42 U.S.C. § 12181.

[3] 28 C.F.R. § 36, App. A (2010).

[4] *Id.*

[5] *See* H.R. 1702, 98th Cong. (1983); *see also* Handicapped Parking Act, H.R. 3889, 99th Cong. (1985) and Handicapped Parking Act, S. 1936, 99th Cong. (1985).

[6] P.L. 100-641, § 3, Nov. 9, 1988, 102 Stat. 3335 (codified as a note at 23 U.S.C. § 402). When introducing the legislation that created the Uniform System, Senator Durenburger stressed "the problems faced by disabled drivers because of State-by-State differences in handicapped parking policies." 134 Cong. Rec. S32031 (daily ed. Oct. 20, 1988) (statement of Sen. Durenberger).

[7] 23 C.F.R. Part 1235 (2010).

[8] At least one later bill proposed legislation that would require states to adopt the federal guidelines. *See* H.R. 2542, 102nd Cong. (1991). However, as amended and adopted, the legislation merely required a study on states' progress in voluntarily adopting the federal guidelines. *See* Intermodal Surface Transportation Efficiency Act of 1991, P.L. 102-240, 105 Stat. 2032 (codified as a note at 23 U.S.C. § 402).

[9] At least one federal court has addressed the issue of whether Congress intended the Uniform System to be merely hortatory. McGarry v. Mo. Dept. of Rev., 7 F.Supp.2d 1022, 1026 (W.D. Mo. 1998). That court held that in contrast to the ADA, the Uniform System is a voluntary program that states can choose to adopt. *Id.*

[10] 23 U.S.C. § 402 (2010).

[11] 23 C.F.R. § 1235.1 (2010).

[12] The ADA definition of "disability" is codified at 42 U.S.C. § 12102, as amended by P.L. 110-325, § 4. For information about the ADA definition, see CRS Report RL34691, *The ADA Amendments Act: P.L. 110-325*, by Nancy Lee Jones.

[13] 23 C.F.R. § 1235.1 (2010). Note that some courts interpreting state statutes which incorporate the Uniform System definition of a person with a disability which impairs or limits the ability to walk have held that this Uniform System definition is no broader than the ADA definition of "disability"; i.e., some courts have held that the Uniform System definition does not apply to individuals who would not otherwise be covered under the ADA. *See, e.g.,* Duprey v. Conn. Dept. of Motor Vehicles, 191 F.R.D. 329, 335-36 (D. Conn. 2000). These cases were based on the ADA definition of "disability" prior to passage of the ADA Amendments Act in 2008. It appears that courts have not yet decided this issue in the context of the amended ADA definition of "disability."

[14] 23 C.F.R. § 1235.2(b) (2010).

[15] *Id.*

[16] The Uniform System defines "special license plate" as "a license plate that displays the International Symbol of Access (1) [i]n a color that contrasts to the background, and (2) [i]n the same size as the letters and/or numbers on the plate." 23 C.F.R. § 1235.2(c) (2010).

[17] 23 C.F.R. § 1235.3(a) (2010); 23 C.F.R. § 1235.4(a) (2010); 23 C.F.R. § 1235.5(a) (2010).

[18] 23 C.F.R. § 1235.3(a) (2010); 23 C.F.R. § 1235.4(b) (2010); 23 C.F.R. § 1235.5(b) (2010).

[19] 23 C.F.R. § 1235.3(c) (2010). Several federal circuit courts have considered the constitutionality of a federal ban on state fees for parking placards, specifically in the context of an ADA regulation prohibiting states from charging fees to cover the cost of accessibility programs. The circuits have reached different conclusions. *Compare* Brown v. North Carolina Div. of Motor Vehicles, 166 F.3d 698, 709-10 (4th Cir. 1999) (upholding the ban) *with* Neinast v. Texas, 217 F.3d 275, 282 (5th Cir. 2000) (holding that the ban "exceeds the scope of Congress' power to abrogate the states' immunity").

[20] 23 C.F.R. § 1235.
6 (2010).

[21] 23 C.F.R. § 1235.5(b) (2010) (requiring physicians' certifications to specify the period of time the individuals will have such an impairment or limitation, "not to exceed six months").

[22] *See* 23 C.F.R. § 1235 (2010) at App. A and App. B.

[23] 23 C.F.R. § 1235.2(a) (2010).

[24] 23 C.F.R. § 1235 (2010) at App. A and App. B.

[25] 23 C.F.R. § 1235.8 (2010).

[26] For more information regarding states' placard designs, see State's Listings of Disabled Placards, License Plates, ID Cards, Motorcycle Plates, http://www.handiplate.com/primary.htm.

[27] *See, e.g.,* Miss. Code Ann. § 27-19-56(1) (2009) (codifying the definition verbatim); Utah Code Ann. § 41-1a-420(3)(a)(i) (2009) (incorporating the Uniform System definition by reference).

[28] *See, e.g.,* Tenn. Code Ann. § 55-21-102 (2009) (defining "disabled driver" as a person who is disabled by paraplegia or amputation, disabled by virtue of having vision not less than 20/200 with correcting glasses, or disabled by "other condition, certified to by a physician duly licensed to practice medicine, resulting in an equal degree of disability . . . so as not to be able to get about without great difficulty").

[29] *See, e.g.,* Ohio Rev. Code Ann. § 4503.44(A)(1)(g) (2009).

[30] *See, e.g.,* Conn. Gen. Stat. § 14-253a(e) (2009); Nev. Rev. Stat. § 484.408(5)(d) (2008).

[31] *See, e.g.,* N.H. Rev. Stat. Ann. § 261.88(IX) (2009).

[32] *See, e.g.,* Mich. Comp. Laws § 257.675(6) (2009) (not incorporating any Uniform System language but providing that "a certificate of identification or windshield placard from another state . . . or special registration plates from another state issued for persons with disabilities is entitled to courtesy in the parking of a vehicle").

[33] N.D. Cent. Code § 39-01-15(11) (2009).

[34] Iowa Code § 321L.2(4) (2009).

[35] *See, e.g.,* Mo. Rev. Stat. § 301.142(11) (2009) (requiring placards to be renewed every four years); Iowa Code § 321L.2(1)(a)(3) (2009) (providing application criteria for "nonexpiring" windshield placards).

INDEX